the traditional
Sunday lunch

the traditional
Sunday lunch

Favourite dishes for family meals, with 70 traditional
starters, main courses and desserts

ANNETTE YATES

HERMES
HOUSE

This edition is published by Hermes House,
an imprint of Anness Publishing Ltd,
Hermes House, 88–89 Blackfriars Road,
London SE1 8HA;
tel. 020 7401 2077; fax 020 7633 9499

www.hermeshouse.com; www.annesspublishing.com

If you like the images in this book and would like to investigate using them for publishing, promotions or advertising, please visit our website www.practicalpictures.com for more information.

Publisher: Joanna Lorenz
Editorial Director: Helen Sudell
Executive Editor: Joanne Rippin
Designer: Nigel Partridge, Jacket design: Adelle Morris
Photographer: Craig Robertson
Food preparation and food styling: Fergal Connelly
Styling and props: Helen Trent

ETHICAL TRADING POLICY

Previously published as part of a larger volume:
England's Heritage Food and Cooking.

PUBLISHER'S NOTE

NOTES

Bracketed terms are intended for American readers.

For all recipes, quantities are given in both metric and imperial measures and, where appropriate, in standard cups and spoons. Follow one set of measures, but not a mixture, because they are not interchangeable.

Standard spoon and cup measures are level. 1 tsp = 5ml, 1 tbsp = 15ml, 1 cup = 250ml/8fl oz. Australian standard tablespoons are 20ml. Australian readers should use 3 tsp in place of 1 tbsp for measuring small quantities.

American pints are 16fl oz/2 cups. American readers should use 20fl oz/2.5 cups in place of 1 pint when measuring liquids.

Electric oven temperatures in this book are for conventional ovens. When using a fan oven, the temperature will probably need to be reduced by about 10–20°C/20–40°F.

Since ovens vary, you should check with your manufacturer's instruction book for guidance.

The nutritional analysis given for each recipe is calculated per portion (i.e. serving or item), unless otherwise stated. If the recipe gives a range, such as Serves 4–6, then the nutritional analysis will be for the smaller portion size, i.e. 6 servings. The analysis does not include optional ingredients, such as salt added to taste. Medium (US large) eggs are used unless otherwise stated.

CONTENTS

Introduction

The simple phrase 'Sunday lunch' paints a picture of a sizzling joint of meat, rich gravy, succulent vegetables and a delicious dessert. This well-loved occasion is said to have originated in medieval times, when the lord of the manor was sometimes good enough to provide a feast for his local militia and farm workers after church and archery practice. In later centuries, Sunday lunch gradually became a ritual – an ideal opportunity to roast a good-sized joint of meat slowly in the oven while the family was at church, followed by frantic activity – cooking vegetables and making gravy – the minute the cook arrived home around midday. The leftovers would feed everyone for days afterwards. To many people, the aroma of roast beef wafting from the kitchen still means 'home' and 'Sunday'.

The family gathering

In these hectic days of the 21st century, it is sometimes difficult to find a time when all the members of a family can sit down to a meal together. Small children and teenagers tend to eat at different times of day from their parents

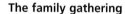

Below Roast beef is still probably the epitome of an English Sunday lunch.

all week, and everyone is busy with all sorts of activities at weekends. But Sunday lunch as a ritual is still thriving, and many families now recognize the value of having dinner together at least once a week. It is an opportunity for adults to catch up with news, for children to learn some social graces, and for everyone to eat a delicious meal with plenty of variety. And for those without an extended family living nearby, Sunday lunch has become an ideal occasion to meet friends for a long, relaxed meal.

Sunday lunch customs

The most typical Sunday lunch consists of a small starter such as soup or potted shrimps, followed by a huge and mouth-watering joint of roast beef, crisp roast potatoes, Yorkshire pudding, plenty of vegetables and lots of gravy. Finally, there must be a stunning dessert of the kind that British cooks have made their speciality – apple pie, fruit crumble, sponge pudding – served with custard or cream.

Above A Sunday lunch benefits from having time not only to prepare the food, but also to enjoy eating it.

However, some great variations on this theme have arisen over the years in various parts of England. Northern cooks tend to serve Yorkshire pudding as a starter – it sits in splendid isolation on the plate with the tasty, meaty gravy poured into the centre. This fills up hungry stomachs and whets the appetite for the rich and costly meat to follow. Lancashire is particularly renowned for its savoury pies and puddings, which eke out a small amount of meat with a lot of gravy and some appetizing pastry. Originally, meat puddings with a suet crust would be boiled in a cloth for several hours – the same length of time as a roast takes to cook and more convenient for those without an oven at home.

Until the 20th century, farming families in the rural areas had access to more meat than their town-dwelling counterparts, and enjoyed roast pork with its crisp crackling during the colder months of the year and tender lamb in the spring. Chicken and turkey are cheap and widely available now, but they were rare a hundred years ago and far more expensive than beef. In those days, poultry dishes were more likely to consist of goose or duck, served frequently at the tables of the rich, but only as an occasional treat for the less affluent. Goose was the traditional roast at Christmas, often roasted in the local baker's oven on Christmas Day.

Alternatives to roast meat

Despite the undeniable fact that fish dishes are not so common as a centrepiece for a big Sunday lunch, there are plenty of time-honoured recipes for cooking a whole salmon or a splendid fish pie for a special occasion. These days the vegetarian option must also be considered. Some vegetarians are happy simply eating all the accompaniments that come with the roast. However, there are plenty of flans and pies that can be served as an alternative main dish with the traditional vegetable side dishes and would satisfy any appetite.

***Below** Often the side dishes, here Brussels sprouts with chestnuts, are as important as the meat they accompany.*

***Above** In summer, roast meat can be substituted with a fine poached salmon.*

The final flourish

The magnificent puddings and desserts that traditionally end a Sunday lunch are usually based either on fruits of the season, for instance apple pie or poached pears, or on creamy mixtures such as rice pudding. Usually everyone can find room for a small bowlful of these delicious concoctions. The trend for eating sweet dishes such as trifle and fruit jelly at the end of a meal started in the 19th century, and Victorian cooks really threw themselves into the task of devising ever more elaborate recipes with wonderful decorations. Nowadays the dishes tend to be simpler, but everyone still looks forward to a seasonal treat such as a beautiful summer pudding or warming winter-fruit crumble.

The recipes in this book

All the dishes described in this book are suitable for a family meal – there is something for everyone to enjoy. The first section gives recipes for starters, which tend to be quite light, leaving room for the serious main course, and

are often made from local, seasonal ingredients or traditionally preserved foods such as smoked fish.

The next section contains a multitude of recipes for the main course and its attendant vegetable dishes. Many of these are completely traditional, including a foolproof recipe for roast beef and Yorkshire pudding. There are savoury pies and stews, as well as the more obvious roast meats, and four crowd-pleasing fish recipes as well. As Sunday lunch would not be complete without a good dessert, the last section of this book concentrates on all the famous dishes that traditionally end a big family meal. There are hot pies and crumbles, cold tarts and trifles, as well as lighter desserts such as jelly and fruit fool.

This book will guide you through the sometimes daunting procedure of making a big Sunday lunch. Each recipe has clear step-by-step instructions so that you can check each stage as you go. You will doubtless find that some dishes become favourites, but if you treat this book as a mix-and-match guide, you can cook a different Sunday lunch every week of the year.

***Below** A traditional English dessert, such as Eve's Pudding, rounds off the classic Sunday lunch.*

Soups and Appetizers

When serving a substantial main course it is wise to avoid filling or heavy starters. A small helping of a well-flavoured soup is perfect for a winter Sunday, or when you are serving a lighter main course such as fish. If you prefer an appetizer to a soup, choose something that will tantilize the tastebuds with well defined flavours, such as smoked fish, salty bacon or a mouthwatering combination of sweet and sour such as the delicious Victorian Devils on Horseback.

Watercress soup

In Roman times, eating watercress was thought to prevent baldness. Later on it became the food of the working classes and was often eaten for breakfast in a sandwich. Watercress has been cultivated in the south of England since the early 19th century, and when it is in season this makes a light, healthy soup to begin Sunday lunch with.

2 Melt the butter in a large pan and add the onion. Cook over a medium heat for about 5 minutes, stirring occasionally, until the onion is soft and just beginning to brown.

3 Stir in the potato and the chopped watercress, then add the stock. Bring to the boil, cover the pan and simmer gently for 15–20 minutes until the potato is very soft.

Serves 6

2 bunches of watercress, about 175g/6oz in total

25g/1oz/2 tbsp butter

1 medium onion, finely chopped

1 medium potato

900ml/1½ pints/3¾ cups chicken or vegetable stock

300ml/½ pint/1¼ cups milk

salt and ground black pepper

single (light) cream, to serve

1 Roughly chop the watercress, reserving a few small sprigs to garnish.

Cook's tip Try adding a little finely grated orange rind and the juice of an orange in step 6.

4 Remove from the heat, leave to cool slightly and then stir in the milk.

5 Process or blend the mixture until the soup is completely smooth.

6 Return the soup to the pan and adjust the seasoning to taste.

7 Reheat gently and top each serving with a spoonful of cream and a few watercress leaves.

Energy 68kcal/280kJ; Protein 1.5g; Carbohydrate 1.4g, of which sugars 1g; Fat 6.3g, of which saturates 2.4g; Cholesterol 8mg; Calcium 79mg; Fibre 0.9g; Sodium 45mg

Celery soup with Stilton

Stilton – known as the "king of English cheeses" – and celery are traditional partners, whether on the cheeseboard or in this tasty soup. The two flavours complement each other beautifully, with the fresh, clean taste of the celery setting off the rich, creamy tang of the cheese. This would make a good foil to a lighter main course, such as poached salmon.

Serves 6

40g/1½oz/3 tbsp butter

1 large onion, finely chopped

1 medium potato, cut into small cubes

1 whole head of celery, thinly sliced

900ml/1½ pints/3¾ cups vegetable or chicken stock

100g/3¾oz Stilton cheese, crumbled

150ml/¼ pint/⅔ cup single (light) cream

salt and ground black pepper

1 Melt the butter in a large pan and add the onion. Cook over a medium heat for 5 minutes, stirring occasionally, until soft but not browned.

2 Stir in the potato and celery and cook for a further 5 minutes until the vegetables soften and begin to brown.

Variation In the place of Stilton try using another cheese, either a blue-veined variety or a strong Cheddar.

3 Add the stock, bring to the boil, then cover the pan and simmer gently for about 30 minutes, until all the vegetables are very soft.

4 Process or blend about three-quarters of the vegetable and stock mixture until smooth, then return it to the pan with the rest of the soup.

5 Bring the soup just to the boil and season to taste with salt and ground black pepper.

6 Remove the pan from the heat and stir in the cheese, reserving a little for the garnish. Stir in the cream and reheat the soup gently without boiling. Serve topped with the reserved cheese.

Energy 199kcal/826kJ; Protein 5.9g; Carbohydrate 7.5g, of which sugars 2.4g; Fat 16.2g, of which saturates 10.4g; Cholesterol 44mg; Calcium 117mg; Fibre 1.4g; Sodium 233mg

Devon crab soup

Although crab is available all the year round, it is at its best and is least expensive during the summer months – the perfect time to make this lovely creamy soup, and it makes an ideal precursor to a summer Sunday main course such as veal and ham pie.

Serves 4–6

25g/1oz/2 tbsp butter

1 medium onion, finely chopped

1 celery stick, finely chopped

1 garlic clove, crushed

25ml/1½ tbsp flour

225g/8oz cooked crab meat, half dark and half white

1.2 litres/2 pints/5 cups fish stock

150ml/¼ pint/⅔ cup double (heavy) cream

30ml/2 tbsp dry sherry

salt and ground black pepper

1 Melt the butter in a pan and add the onion, celery and garlic. Cook over a medium heat for about 5 minutes, stirring frequently, until the vegetables are soft but not browned.

2 Remove from the heat and quickly stir in the flour, then the brown crab meat. Gradually stir in the stock.

3 Bring the mixture just to the boil, then reduce the heat and simmer for about 30 minutes. Process or blend the soup and return it to the cleaned pan. Season to taste with salt and pepper.

4 Chop the white crab meat and stir it into the pan with the cream and sherry. Reheat the soup and serve immediately.

Energy 209kcal/867kJ; Protein 7.8g; Carbohydrate 4.6g, of which sugars 1.2g; Fat 17.3g, of which saturates 10.6g; Cholesterol 70mg; Calcium 69mg; Fibre 0.3g; Sodium 241mg

Smoked mackerel pâté

The south-west of England and East Anglia in particular are known for smoking fish, especially freshly caught mackerel. This modern recipe provides an ideal way to use smoked mackerel – it's quick and easy, and is the perfect light but tasty starter to a large lunch.

Serves 4–6

225g/8oz/1 cup crème fraîche or Greek (US strained plain) yogurt

finely grated rind of ½ lemon

few sprigs of parsley

225g/8oz smoked mackerel fillets

5–10ml/1–2 tsp horseradish sauce

1 tbsp lemon juice, or to taste

ground black pepper

crusty bread, hot toast or crisp plain crackers, to serve

lemon wedges, to serve

1 Put the crème fraîche and lemon rind into a blender or food processor. Add a few sprigs of parsley.

2 Flake the mackerel, discarding the skin and any bones. Add the flaked fish to the blender. Blend on a medium speed until almost smooth.

3 Add the horseradish sauce and lemon juice and blend briefly. Season with pepper. Spoon into individual dishes. Cover and refrigerate until required.

4 Garnish with parsley and serve with crusty bread, hot toast or crackers and lemon wedges for squeezing over.

Energy 344kcal/1421kJ; Protein 10.7g; Carbohydrate 0.5g, of which sugars 0.4g; Fat 33.3g, of which saturates 14.3g; Cholesterol 88mg; Calcium 57mg; Fibre 0.1g; Sodium 518mg

Salmon mousse

This type of light and delicate mousse often features in the wedding feasts of English brides. It is ideal for a summer Sunday lunch, garnished with thinly sliced cucumber, cherry tomatoes and lemon wedges. Serve it with something crisp – thin crackers or toast.

Serves 6–8

300ml/½ pint/1¼ cups milk

1 small onion, thinly sliced

1 small carrot, thinly sliced

2 bay leaves

2 sprigs of parsley or dill

4 whole peppercorns

15ml/1 tbsp powdered gelatine

350g/12oz salmon fillet

75ml/5 tbsp dry white vermouth or white wine

25g/1oz/2 tbsp butter

25g/1oz/4 tbsp flour

75ml/5 tbsp mayonnaise

150ml/¼ pint/⅔ cup whipping cream

salt and ground black pepper

1 Put the milk in a pan with half the onion, carrot, herbs and peppercorns. Bring slowly to the boil, remove from the heat, cover and leave to stand for 30 minutes to infuse. Meanwhile, sprinkle the gelatine over 45ml/3 tbsp cold water and leave to soak.

2 Put the salmon in a pan with the remaining onion, carrot, herbs and peppercorns. Add the vermouth and 60ml/4 tbsp water. Simmer, covered, for 10 minutes. Flake the fish, discarding the skin and bones. Boil the juices in the pan to reduce by half, strain and reserve.

3 Strain the infused milk into a clean pan and add the butter and flour. Whisking continuously, cook until the sauce thickens, then simmer gently for 1 minute. Pour into a food processor or blender. Add the soaked gelatine and blend. Add the salmon and the reserved cooking juices and blend briefly.

4 Tip into a bowl and stir in the mayonnaise and seasonings. Whip the cream and fold in gently. Pour into an oiled mould, cover and refrigerate for about 2 hours or until set. Turn the mousse out onto a flat plate to serve.

Energy 285kcal/1183kJ; Protein 12.6g; Carbohydrate 5.8g, of which sugars 3.2g; Fat 22.7g, of which saturates 8.7g; Cholesterol 57mg; Calcium 73mg; Fibre 0.2g; Sodium 103mg

Potted shrimps

Tiny brown shrimps found in the seas around England (most famously those from Morecambe Bay) have been potted in spiced butter since about 1800. If your fishmonger doesn't have them you can use small cooked prawns instead.

Serves 4

225g/8oz cooked, shelled shrimps

225g/8oz/1 cup butter

pinch of ground mace

salt

cayenne pepper

dill sprigs, to garnish

lemon wedges and thin slices of brown bread and butter, to serve

1 Chop a quarter of the shrimps. Melt 115g/4oz/½ cup of the butter slowly.

2 Skim off any foam that rises to the surface of the butter. Stir in all the shrimps, the mace, salt and cayenne and heat gently without boiling. Pour the mixture into four individual dishes and leave to cool.

3 Melt the remaining butter in a small pan, then spoon the clear butter over the shrimps, leaving the sediment behind. When the butter is almost set, place a dill sprig in the centre of each dish. Cover and chill.

4 Remove from the refrigerator 30 minutes before serving with lemon wedges and brown bread and butter.

Prawn cocktail

This 1960s dinner-party appetizer is a delight, so long as it includes really crisp lettuce and is assembled at the last minute. The traditional accompaniment is brown bread and butter.

Serves 6

60ml/4 tbsp double (heavy) cream, lightly whipped

60ml/4 tbsp mayonnaise

60ml/4 tbsp tomato ketchup

5–10ml/1–2 tsp Worcestershire sauce

juice of 1 lemon

450g/1lb cooked peeled prawns (shrimp)

½ crisp lettuce, finely shredded

salt, ground black pepper and paprika

thinly sliced brown bread, butter and lemon wedges, to serve

1 Mix the cream, mayonnaise, ketchup, Worcestershire sauce and lemon juice in a bowl. Stir in the prawns and season.

2 Part-fill six glasses with lettuce. Spoon the prawns over and sprinkle with paprika. Serve immediately.

Energy 460kcal/1895kJ; Protein 9.6g; Carbohydrate 0.4g, of which sugars 0.4g; Fat 46.7g, of which saturates 29.4g; Cholesterol 193mg; Calcium 83mg; Fibre 0g; Sodium 555mg

Energy 193kcal/802kJ; Protein 13.9g; Carbohydrate 4g, of which sugars 3.9g; Fat 13.6g, of which saturates 4.6g; Cholesterol 167mg; Calcium 79mg; Fibre 0.4g; Sodium 374mg

Angels on horseback

This recipe dates back to the 19th century, when oysters were plentiful and cheap. It became fashionable in England to serve a savoury – a small, strongly flavoured dish – at the end of a meal, mainly to revive the palates of the gentlemen after dessert and before the arrival of the port. Nowadays, this little dish makes a delicious appetizer with drinks.

Serves 4

16 oysters, removed from their shells

fresh lemon juice

8 rindless rashers (strips) of lean streaky (fatty) bacon

8 small slices of bread

butter, for spreading

paprika (optional)

1 Preheat the oven to 200°C/400°F/ Gas 6. Sprinkle the oysters with a little lemon juice.

2 Lay the bacon rashers on a board, slide the back of a knife along each one to stretch it and then cut it in half crosswise. Wrap a piece of bacon around each oyster and secure with a wooden cocktail stick (toothpick). Arrange them on a baking sheet.

3 Put the oysters and bacon into the hot oven for 8–10 minutes until the bacon is just cooked through.

4 Meanwhile, toast the bread. When the bacon is cooked, butter the hot toast and serve the bacon-wrapped oysters on top. Sprinkle with a little paprika, if using.

Devils on horseback

This is another popular savoury, designed to be served at the end of a lavish dinner, that makes a good appetizer. The prunes are sometimes filled with paté, olives, almonds or nuggets of cured meat. Serve with some chilled white wine before the roast is served.

Serves 4

16 stoned prunes

fruit chutney, such as mango

8 rindless rashers (strips) of lean streaky bacon

8 small slices of bread

butter for spreading

1 Preheat the oven to 200°C/400°F/ Gas 6. Ease open the prunes and spoon a small amount of fruit chutney into each cavity.

2 Lay the bacon rashers on a board, slide the back of a knife along each one to stretch it and then cut in half crosswise. Wrap a piece of bacon around each prune and lay them close together (if they touch each other, they are less likely to unroll during cooking) on a baking sheet.

3 Put into the hot oven for 8–10 minutes until the bacon is cooked through.

4 Meanwhile, toast the bread. Butter the hot toast and serve the bacon-wrapped prunes on top.

Energy 326kcal/1365kJ; Protein 20.3g; Carbohydrate 26.4g, of which sugars 1.4g; Fat 16.2g, of which saturates 6.9g; Cholesterol 79mg; Calcium 147mg; Fibre 0.8g; Sodium 1483mg

Energy 309kcal/1303kJ; Protein 14.7g; Carbohydrate 41.7g, of which sugars 18.3g; Fat 10.4g, of which saturates 3.5g; Cholesterol 30mg; Calcium 75mg; Fibre 3.6g; Sodium 1132mg

Salad with warm black pudding

Black pudding is a traditional sausage containing pig's blood that is flavoured with spices. In England it is considered a Lancashire speciality, but similar sausages are also found all over Britain, particularly in the Midlands. Fried rapidly so that the outside is crisp, and the inside still moist, slices of black pudding are delicious in this quick and easy starter.

Serves 4

250g/9oz black pudding (blood sausage)

45ml/3 tbsp olive oil

1 small crusty loaf, plain or flavoured with herbs, cut into small chunks

1 Romaine lettuce, torn into bite size pieces

250g/9oz cherry tomatoes, halved

For the dressing

juice of 1 lemon

90ml/6 tbsp olive oil

5ml/1 tsp English (hot) mustard

15ml/1 tbsp clear honey

30ml/2 tbsp chopped fresh herbs, such as chives and parsley

salt and ground black pepper

1 Slice the black pudding with a sharp knife, then dry-fry the slices on both sides over a medium heat in a non-stick frying pan for 5–10 minutes, until crisp.

2 Remove the black pudding from the pan using a slotted spoon and drain the slices on kitchen paper. Keep warm.

3 Mix together the ingredients for the salad dressing and season to taste with salt and pepper.

4 Add the olive oil to the juices in the frying pan and cook the bread cubes in two batches, turning often, until golden on all sides. Drain the croûtons on kitchen paper.

5 Mix together the croûtons, black pudding, lettuce and cherry tomatoes in a large bowl. Pour the dressing over the salad, mix well and serve at once.

Variation Try this salad with pieces of bacon, fried until crispy, or chunks of grilled, herby sausages in place of the black pudding.

Energy 683kcal/2858kJ; Protein 16.4g; Carbohydrate 66.5g, of which sugars 9.5g; Fat 41g, of which saturates 9g; Cholesterol 43mg; Calcium 234mg; Fibre 3.5g; Sodium 1156mg

Pears with Stilton and walnuts

English cheeses and fruit taste wonderful together. This dish needs pears that are fully ripe and juicy, yet firm. It makes a good starter for a large lunch as it is quick and easy to assemble, and isn't too filling for the start of a three-course meal.

Serves 6

115g/4oz/½ cup cream cheese or curd cheese

75g/3oz Stilton cheese

30–45ml/2–3 tbsp single (light) cream

115g/4oz/1 cup roughly chopped walnuts

6 ripe pears

15ml/1 tbsp lemon juice

mixed salad leaves

6 cherry tomatoes

salt and ground black pepper

walnut halves and sprigs of fresh flat-leaf parsley, to garnish

For the dressing

juice of 1 lemon

a little finely grated lemon rind

pinch of caster (superfine) sugar

60ml/4 tbsp olive oil

1 Mash the cream cheese and Stilton together with a good grinding of black pepper, then blend in the cream to make a smooth mixture. Stir in 25g/1oz/¼ cup chopped walnuts. Cover the mixture and chill until required.

2 Peel and halve the pears lengthways and scoop out the cores. Put them into a bowl of cold water with the lemon juice to prevent them from browning. Whisk the dressing ingredients together and season to taste.

3 Divide the salad leaves between six plates – shallow soup plates are ideal – add a tomato to each and sprinkle over the remaining chopped walnuts.

4 Drain the pears well and pat dry with kitchen paper, then turn them in the prepared dressing and arrange, hollow side up, on the salad. Pile the cheese mixture into the pears and spoon over the rest of the dressing. Garnish with walnut halves and flat leaf parsley.

Variation Try other blue cheeses such as Beenleigh Blue or Oxford Blue, or for a milder taste use soft cream cheese.

Energy 407kcal/1684kJ; Protein 7.1g; Carbohydrate 16.7g, of which sugars 16.6g; Fat 34.9g, of which saturates 11.3g; Cholesterol 33mg; Calcium 100mg; Fibre 4.1g; Sodium 164mg

Potted cheese

The potting of cheese became popular in the 18th century, and it is still a great way to use up odd pieces left on the cheeseboard. Blend them with your chosen seasonings, adjusting the flavour before adding the alcohol. Serve with plain crackers, oatcakes or crisp toast.

Serves 4–6

250g/9oz hard cheese, such as mature Cheddar

75g/3oz/6 tbsp soft unsalted butter, plus extra for melting

1.5ml/¼ tsp ready-made English (hot) mustard

1.5ml/¼ tsp ground mace

30ml/2 tbsp sherry

ground black pepper

fresh parsley, to garnish

1 Cut the cheese into rough pieces and put them into the bowl of a food processor. Use the pulse button to chop the cheese into small crumbs.

2 Add the butter, mustard, mace and a little black pepper and blend again until smooth. Taste and adjust the seasoning. Finally, blend in the sherry.

3 Spoon the mixture into a dish just large enough to leave about 1cm/½in to spare on top. Level the surface.

Variations Use some crumbled Stilton in place of the Cheddar and the same quantity of port in place of sherry.
• Some finely chopped chives could be added instead of mustard.

4 Melt some butter in a small pan, skimming off any foam that rises to the surface. Leaving the sediment in the pan, pour a layer of melted butter on top of the cheese mixture to cover the surface. Refrigerate until required.

5 Garnish with parsley and serve spread on thin slices of toast or crispbread.

Energy 262kcal/1082kJ; Protein 10.7g; Carbohydrate 0.2g, of which sugars 0.2g; Fat 23.6g, of which saturates 15.2g; Cholesterol 70mg; Calcium 290mg; Fibre 0g; Sodium 363mg

Main Courses

England takes great pride in its Sunday roast;
a succulent joint of beef, lamb or pork cooked to
perfection in the oven and served with all the
trimmings. Then there are pot roasts, stews and
braises, puddings and pies, not to mention bacon,
chops and steaks to grill, pan-fry or bake. Vegetables
dishes are also important, and this chapter offers a
selection of popular accompaniments.

Poached salmon with hollandaise sauce

Though it was once plentiful, wild salmon is now a rare and expensive treat, but farmed fish is widely available. A whole poached fish makes an elegant Sunday lunch dish, especially on a hot summer day, served with new potatoes and a green salad.

Serves 8–10

300ml/½ pint/1¼ cups dry (hard) cider or white wine

1 large carrot, roughly chopped

2 medium onions, roughly chopped

2 celery sticks, roughly chopped

2 bay leaves

a few black peppercorns

sprig of parsley

sprig of thyme

2–2.5kg/4½–5½lb whole salmon, gutted, washed and dried

For the hollandaise sauce

175g/6oz/¾ cup unsalted butter

5ml/1 tsp sugar

3 egg yolks

10ml/2 tsp cider vinegar or white wine vinegar

10ml/2 tsp lemon juice

salt and ground white pepper

1 Put all the ingredients except the salmon into a large pan and add 1 litre/1¾ pints/4 cups water. Bring to the boil and simmer gently for 30–40 minutes. Strain and leave to cool.

2 About 30 minutes before serving, pour the cooled stock into a fish kettle. Lay the salmon on the rack and lower it into the liquid.

3 Slowly heat the kettle until the stock almost comes to the boil (with small bubbles forming and rising to the surface), cover and simmer very gently for 20–25 minutes until the fish is just cooked through – test the thickest part with a knife near the backbone.

4 Meanwhile, to make the hollandaise sauce, heat the butter with the sugar (on the stove or in the microwave) until the butter has melted and the mixture is hot but not sizzling – do not allow it to brown.

5 Put the egg yolks, vinegar, lemon juice and seasonings into a processor or blender and blend on high speed for about 15 seconds, or until the mixture is creamy.

6 Keep the processor or blender on high speed and add the hot butter mixture in a slow stream until the sauce is thick, smooth and creamy.

7 Lift the salmon out of its cooking liquid. Remove the skin carefully, so the flesh remains intact, and lift the salmon on to a warmed serving plate. Garnish with watercress and serve with the warm hollandaise.

Variation To cook salmon that is to be served cold, in step 3 slowly heat until the stock just comes to the boil, let it bubble two or three times then cover, remove from the heat and leave to cool completely (this will take up to 12 hours). When cold, lift out the fish and slide it on to a serving plate. Strip off the fins and peel away the skin and garnish with wafer-thin cucumber slices arranged like scales, salad leaves, baby tomatoes or black olives. Serve the salmon with mayonnaise.

Energy 450kcal/1868kJ; Protein 34.6g; Carbohydrate 0.5g, of which sugars 0.5g; Fat 34.4g, of which saturates 12.8g; Cholesterol 182mg; Calcium 44mg; Fibre 0g; Sodium 183mg

Pan-fried Dover sole

For non-meat eaters, or to make a change from the traditional roast, try this delicious fish dish as a main course. It is ideal for when you just can't spend the whole morning cooking.

2 Add one or two fish to the pan and cook over a medium heat for 3–5 minutes on each side until golden brown and cooked through. Lift them out and keep them warm while you cook the remaining fish.

3 Add the remaining oil and the butter to the hot pan and heat until the butter has melted. Stir in the lemon juice and chopped herbs. Drizzle the pan juices over the fish and serve immediately, garnished with watercress sprigs.

Cook's tips Leaving the white skin on one side of the fish helps to keep its shape during cooking; it is also full of flavour and good to eat, particularly the crisp edges.
• To grill (broil) the fish, omit the flour coating and brush both sides with melted butter. Put the sole under a medium-hot grill (broiler) and cook for 5–7 minutes on each side until golden brown and cooked through.

Serves 4

4 small Dover sole, dark skin and fins removed

30–45ml/2–3 tbsp flour seasoned with salt and pepper

45ml/3 tbsp olive oil

25g/1oz/2 tbsp butter

juice of 1 lemon

15ml/1 tbsp chopped fresh herbs

watercress sprigs, to garnish

1 Spread the seasoned flour on a plate, and coat each fish, shaking off any excess. Heat a large non-stick frying pan and add the oil.

Energy 177kcal/739kJ; Protein 18.6g; Carbohydrate 3g, of which sugars 0.2g; Fat 10.2g, of which saturates 1.2g; Cholesterol 50mg; Calcium 42mg; Fibre 0.3g; Sodium 101mg

Trout with almonds

Another classic English fish recipe that makes a fresh, simple alternative to a meat main course. Trout's earthy flavour goes particularly well with buttery juices and toasted almonds.

Serves 4

4 whole trout, cleaned

45–60ml/3–4 tbsp seasoned flour,

75g/3oz/6 tbsp butter

15ml/1 tbsp olive oil

50g/2oz/½ cup flaked (sliced) almonds

juice of ½ lemon

lemon wedges, to serve

1 Wash the fish, dry with kitchen paper and coat them with seasoned flour, shaking off any excess.

2 Heat half the butter with the oil in a large frying pan. When the mixture begins to foam, add one or two fish.

3 Cook over medium heat for 3–5 minutes on each side or until golden brown and cooked through. Lift out, drain on kitchen paper and keep warm.

4 Cook the remaining fish, then wipe the pan out with kitchen paper. Add the remaining butter and when foaming add the almonds. Cook gently, stirring frequently, until the almonds are golden brown. Remove from the heat and add the lemon juice.

5 Sprinkle the almonds and pan juices over the trout and serve immediately with lemon wedges for squeezing over.

Cook's tip When buying the trout, choose a size that will fit inside your frying pan.

Variation The trout can be grilled (broiled) if preferred. Omit the flour coating. Melt half the butter and brush over both sides of the fish. Put the fish under a medium-hot grill (broiler) and cook for 5–7 minutes on each side until golden brown and cooked all the way through. Cook the almonds in butter as in step 4 above.

Energy 475kcal/1978kJ; Protein 39.2g; Carbohydrate 7.6g, of which sugars 0.8g; Fat 32.2g, of which saturates 12.4g; Cholesterol 187mg; Calcium 101mg; Fibre 1.2g; Sodium 249mg

Fisherman's casserole

Another ideal choice for non-meat eaters, this fish casserole makes a delicious centrepiece for a Sunday lunch. It is important to serve as soon as the casserole is ready, so that the fish doesn't overcook; finish cooking this while your guests nibble at appetizers.

Serves 4

500g/1¼lb mixed fish fillets, such as haddock, bass, red mullet, salmon

500g/1¼lb mixed shellfish, such as squid strips, mussels, cockles and prawns (shrimp)

15ml/1 tbsp oil

25g/1oz/2 tbsp butter

1 medium onion, finely chopped

1 carrot, finely chopped

3 celery sticks, finely chopped

30ml/2 tbsp plain (all-purpose) flour

600ml/1 pint/2½ cups fish stock

300ml/½pt/1¼ cups dry (hard) cider

350g/12oz small new potatoes, halved

150m/¼ pint/⅔ cup double (heavy) cream

small handful of chopped mixed herbs such as parsley, chives and dill

salt and ground black pepper

1 Wash the fish fillets and dry on kitchen paper. With a sharp knife, remove the skin, feel carefully for any bones and extract them. Cut the fish into large, even chunks.

2 Prepare the shellfish, shelling the prawns if necessary. Scrub the mussels and cockles, discarding any with broken shells or that do not close when given a sharp tap. Pull off the black tufts (beards) attached to the mussels.

3 Heat the oil and butter in a large saucepan, add the onion, carrot and celery and cook over a medium heat, stirring occasionally, until beginning to soften and turn golden brown. Add the flour, and cook for 1 minute.

4 Remove the pan from the heat and gradually stir in the fish stock and cider. Return the pan to the heat and cook, stirring continuously, until the mixture comes to the boil and thickens.

Cook's tip This simple recipe can be adapted according to the varieties of fish and shellfish that are obtainable on the day – it is delicious whatever mixture you choose.

5 Add the potatoes. Bring the sauce back to the boil, then cover and simmer gently for 10–15 minutes until the potatoes are nearly tender.

6 Add all the fish and shellfish and stir in gently.

7 Stir in the cream. Bring back to a gentle simmer, then cover the pan and cook gently for 5–10 minutes or until the pieces of fish are cooked through and all the shells have opened. Adjust the seasoning to taste and gently stir in the herbs. Serve immediately.

Energy 583kcal/2439kJ; Protein 49.3g; Carbohydrate 25.3g, of which sugars 6.1g; Fat 30.2g, of which saturates 16.5g; Cholesterol 354mg; Calcium 199mg; Fibre 2.5g; Sodium 404mg

Rib of beef with Yorkshire puddings

Mention English food and most people think of this quintessential dish, which is almost exclusively served for Sunday lunch. In Victorian days in the north-east of England, roast beef would have been traditional fare on Christmas Day. The accompanying batter pudding was not served alongside it until well into the 18th century and in Yorkshire it is still sometimes eaten with gravy before the meat course.

Serves 6–8

rib of beef joint, weighing about 3kg/6½lb

oil, for brushing

salt and ground black pepper

For the Yorkshire puddings

115g/4oz/1 cup plain (all-purpose) flour

1.5ml/¼ tsp salt

1 egg

200ml/7fl oz/scant 1 cup milk

oil or beef dripping, for greasing

For the horseradish cream

60–75ml/4–5 tbsp finely grated fresh horseradish

300ml/½ pint/1¼ cups soured cream

30ml/2 tbsp cider vinegar or white wine vinegar

10ml/2 tsp caster (superfine) sugar

For the gravy

600ml/1 pint/2½ cups good beef stock

1 Preheat the oven to 220°C/425°F/ Gas 7. Weigh the joint and calculate the cooking time required as follows: 10–15 minutes per 500g/1¼lb for rare beef, 15–20 minutes for medium and 20–25 minutes for well done.

Cook's tip To avoid the pungent smell (and tears) produced by grating horseradish, use a jar of preserved grated horseradish.

2 Put the joint into a large roasting pan. Brush it all over with oil and season with salt and pepper. Put into the hot oven and cook for 30 minutes, until the beef is browned. Lower the oven temperature to 160°C/325°F/Gas 3 and cook for the calculated time, spooning the juices over the meat occasionally during cooking.

3 For the Yorkshire pudding, sift the flour and salt into a bowl and break the egg into it. Make the milk up to 300ml/½ pint/1¼ cups with water and gradually whisk into the flour to make a smooth batter. Leave to stand while the beef cooks. Generously grease eight Yorkshire pudding tins (muffin pans) measuring about 10cm/4in.

4 For the horseradish cream, put all the ingredients into a bowl and mix well. Cover and chill until required.

5 At the end of its cooking time, remove the beef from the oven, cover with foil and leave to stand for 30–40 minutes while you cook the Yorkshire puddings and make the gravy.

6 Increase the oven temperature to 220°C/425°F/Gas 7 and put the prepared tins on the top shelf for 5 minutes until very hot. Pour in the batter and cook for about 15 minutes until well risen, crisp and golden brown.

7 To make the gravy, transfer the beef to a warmed serving plate. Pour off the fat from the roasting pan, leaving the meat juices. Add the stock to the pan, bring to the boil and bubble until reduced by about half. Season to taste.

8 Carve the beef and serve with the gravy, Yorkshire puddings, roast potatoes and horseradish cream.

Energy 1037kcal/4338kJ; Protein 129g; Carbohydrate 15.1g, of which sugars 4.1g; Fat 51.5g, of which saturates 24.3g; Cholesterol 352mg; Calcium 123mg; Fibre 0.5g; Sodium 249mg

Pot-roasted beef with stout

This method is ideal for cuts that need tenderizing by long, slow cooking. It makes the perfect dish for a busy Sunday, and can safely simmer in the oven while you are occupied.

Serves 6

30ml/2 tbsp vegetable oil

900g/2lb rolled brisket of beef

2 medium onions, roughly chopped

2 celery sticks, thickly sliced

450g/1lb carrots, cut into large chunks

675g/1½lb potatoes, peeled and cut into large chunks

30ml/2 tbsp plain (all-purpose) flour

450ml/¾ pint/ 2 cups beef stock

300ml/½ pint/1¼ cups stout

1 bay leaf

45ml/3 tbsp chopped fresh thyme

5ml/1 tsp soft light brown sugar

30ml/2 tbsp wholegrain mustard

15ml/1 tbsp tomato purée (paste)

salt and ground black pepper

3 Add the celery, carrots and potatoes to the casserole and cook over a medium heat for 2–3 minutes, or until they are just beginning to colour.

4 Add the flour and cook for a further 1 minute, stirring continuously. Gradually pour in the beef stock and the stout. Heat until the mixture comes to the boil, stirring frequently.

5 Stir in the bay leaf, thyme, sugar, mustard, tomato purée and seasoning. Place the meat on top, cover tightly and transfer the casserole to the hot oven.

6 Cook for about 2½ hours, or until the tender. Adjust the seasoning, to taste. To serve, carve the beef into thick slices and serve with the vegetables and plenty of gravy.

1 Preheat the oven to 180°C/350°F/ Gas 4. Heat the oil in a large flameproof casserole and brown the beef until golden brown all over.

2 Lift the beef from the pan and drain on kitchen paper. Add the onions to the pan and cook for about 4 minutes, until just beginning to soften and brown.

Energy 415kcal/1743kJ; Protein 36g; Carbohydrate 35.6g, of which sugars 13.1g; Fat 14g, of which saturates 4.4g; Cholesterol 81mg; Calcium 66mg; Fibre 4.2g; Sodium 284mg

Braised beef with herb dumplings

Another dish that cooks by itself, perfect for a busy Sunday. Dumplings have been added to English stews for centuries, and this casserole makes a lovely, warming winter lunch.

Serves 4

25g/1oz/2 tbsp butter

30ml/2 tbsp oil

115g/4oz/⅔ cup streaky (fatty) bacon, chopped

900g/2lb lean braising steak, cut into chunks

45ml/3 tbsp plain (all-purpose) flour

450ml/¾ pint/scant 2 cups beer

450ml/¾ pint/scant 2 cups beef stock

1 bouquet garni

8 shallots

175g/6oz/2 cups small mushrooms

salt and ground black pepper

For the herb dumplings

115g/4oz/1 cup self-raising (self-rising) flour

50g/2oz/scant ½ cup shredded suet

2.5ml/½ tsp salt

2.5ml/½ tsp mustard powder

15ml/1 tbsp chopped fresh parsley

15ml/1 tbsp fresh thyme leaves

1 In a large frying pan, melt half the butter with half the oil, add the bacon and brown. Transfer to a casserole.

2 Brown the beef quickly in the frying pan in batches, then transfer it to the casserole using a slotted spoon.

3 Stir the flour into the fat in the pan. Add the beer, stock and seasoning and bring to the boil, stirring constantly. Pour over the meat, add the bouquet garni, cover and place in a cold oven set to 200°C/400°F/Gas 6. Cook for 30 minutes then reduce the temperature to 160°C/325°F/Gas 3 and cook for 1 hour.

4 Heat the remaining butter and oil in a frying pan and cook the shallots until golden. Lift out and set aside. Add the mushrooms and cook quickly for 2–3 minutes. Stir the vegetables into the stew, cover and cook for 30 minutes.

5 In a bowl, mix together the dumpling ingredients. Add cold water to make a soft, sticky dough. Roll into 12 balls and place on top of the stew. Cover, cook for a further 25 minutes, and serve.

Energy 754kcal/3148kJ; Protein 60.8g; Carbohydrate 36.6g, of which sugars 3.8g; Fat 41.4g, of which saturates 14.9g; Cholesterol 163mg; Calcium 147mg; Fibre 2.1g; Sodium 700mg

Braised sausages

Usually known more as a supper dish, these braised sausages are also great for a family Sunday lunch. Choose your favourite good-quality sausages, such as traditional pork, Cumberland, or something more unusual, such as duck, venison or wild boar.

Serves 4

30ml/2 tbsp oil

8 meaty sausages

2 onions, sliced

15ml/1 tbsp plain (all-purpose) flour

400ml/14fl oz/1⅔ cups dry (hard) cider

350g/12oz celeriac, cut into chunks

15ml/1 tbsp Worcestershire sauce

15ml/1 tbsp chopped fresh sage

2 small cooking apples

salt and ground black pepper

1 Preheat the oven to 180°C/350°F/ Gas 4. Heat the oil in a frying pan, add the sausages and fry for about 5 minutes until evenly browned.

2 Transfer the sausages to an ovenproof cassserole dish and drain any excess oil from the pan to leave 15ml/1 tbsp. Add the onions and cook for a few minutes, stirring occasionally, until softened and turning golden.

3 Stir in the flour, then gradually add the cider and bring to the boil, stirring. Add the celeriac and stir in the Worcestershire sauce and sage. Season with salt and black pepper.

4 Pour the cider and celeriac mixture over the sausages. Cover, put into the hot oven and cook for 30 minutes, or until the celeriac is soft.

5 Quarter the apples, remove their cores and cut into thick slices. Stir the apple slices into the casserole, cover and cook for a further 10–15 minutes, or until the apples are just tender. Taste and adjust the seasoning if necessary before serving.

Energy 508kcal/2114kJ; Protein 12.7g; Carbohydrate 29.3g, of which sugars 13.6g; Fat 35.8g, of which saturates 12.3g; Cholesterol 45mg; Calcium 131mg; Fibre 3.3g; Sodium 1019mg

Liver and bacon casserole

Instead of the long, slow cooking of a traditional casserole, this dish of lamb's liver and bacon is cooked in less than half an hour. You could, of course, cook calf's or pig's liver in the same way. Baby potatoes and green beans make ideal accompaniments.

Serves 4

30ml/2 tbsp olive oil

225g/8oz rindless unsmoked lean bacon rashers (strips), cut into pieces

2 onions, halved and sliced

175g/6oz/2 cups mushrooms, halved

450g/1lb lamb's liver, sliced

25g/1oz/2 tbsp butter

15ml/1 tbsp soy sauce

30ml/2 tbsp plain (all-purpose) flour

150ml/¼ pint/⅔ cup hot, well-flavoured chicken stock

salt and ground black pepper

1 Heat the oil in a frying pan, add the bacon and fry until crisp.

2 Add the sliced onions and cook for about 10 minutes, stirring frequently, until softened and turning golden. Add the mushrooms to the pan and cook for a further 1 minute.

3 Using a slotted spoon, remove the bacon and vegetables from the pan and keep warm.

4 Add the liver to the fat remaining in the pan and cook over a high heat for 3–4 minutes, turning once, until browned on both sides. Remove the liver from the pan and keep warm.

5 Melt the butter in the pan, add the soy sauce and flour and blend together. Gradually stir in the stock and bring to the boil, stirring until thickened. Return the liver, bacon and vegetables to the pan and stir into the gravy. Heat through for 1 minute, season to taste and serve immediately.

Energy 431kcal/1796kJ; Protein 34.7g; Carbohydrate 12.3g, of which sugars 6.1g; Fat 27.4g, of which saturates 9.4g; Cholesterol 527mg; Calcium 46mg; Fibre 2g; Sodium 1259mg

Venison stew

Once the preserve of nobility, venison is now a popular meat, lean and full of flavour. This simple yet deeply flavoured stew combines the dark, rich meat of venison with red wine, sweet redcurrant jelly and bacon. Serve it with mashed potato and green vegetables.

Serves 4

1.3kg/3lb stewing venison (shoulder or topside), trimmed and cut into chunks

50g/2oz/4 tbsp butter

225g/8oz piece of streaky (fatty) bacon, cut into 2cm/¾in cubes

2 large onions, chopped

1 large carrot, chopped

1 large garlic clove, crushed

30ml/2 tbsp plain (all-purpose) flour

½ bottle red wine, about 350ml/12fl oz/1½ cups

300ml/½ pint/1¼ cups dark stock

1 bay leaf

sprig of fresh thyme

200g/7oz button (white) mushrooms, sliced

30ml/2 tbsp redcurrant jelly

salt and ground black pepper

1 Dry the venison thoroughly using kitchen paper and set aside.

2 Melt the butter in a large, heavy pan then cook the bacon pieces over a medium-high heat, stirring occasionally, until starting to brown. Reduce the heat to medium, add the onions and carrot and cook until the vegetables are lightly browned, stirring occasionally.

3 Add the pieces of venison to the pan together with the garlic and stir into the mixture. Sprinkle on the flour and mix well until it has been absorbed by the fat in the pan.

4 Pour in the wine and sufficient dark stock to cover. Add the fresh herbs, mushrooms and redcurrant jelly.

5 Cover the pan and simmer gently over a low heat for about 1½–2 hours until the meat is cooked.

Cook's tip This dish can be cooked in advance and left for a couple of days in the refrigerator, which will enhance the flavour. Simply reheat, slowly, adding a little wine if necessary, before serving.

Variation Use good-quality lean beef in place of venison.

Energy 727kcal/3045kJ; Protein 83.8g; Carbohydrate 17.5g, of which sugars 14.4g; Fat 31.3g, of which saturates 13.8g; Cholesterol 226mg; Calcium 70mg; Fibre 2.9g; Sodium 985mg

Roast shoulder of lamb with mint sauce

Lamb is one of the popular meat choices that are traditionally roasted and served on Sundays. It is particularly popular at Easter. Mint sauce, with its sweet-sour combination, has been lamb's customary accompaniment since at least the 17th century.

Serves 6–8

For the mint sauce

large handful of fresh mint leaves

15ml/1 tbsp caster (superfine) sugar

45–60ml/3–4 tbsp cider vinegar or wine vinegar

boned shoulder of lamb, weighing 1.5–2kg/3¼–4½lb

30ml/2 tbsp fresh thyme leaves

30ml/2 tbsp clear honey

150ml/¼ pint/⅔ cup dry (hard) cider or white wine

30–45ml/2–3 tbsp double (heavy) cream (optional)

salt and ground black pepper

1 Preheat the oven to 220°C/425°F/ Gas 7. To make the mint sauce, finely chop the mint leaves with the sugar (the sugar draws the juices from the mint) and put the mixture into a bowl.

2 Add 30ml/2 tbsp boiling water (from the kettle) to the mint and sugar, and stir well until the sugar has dissolved. Add the vinegar to taste and leave the sauce to stand for at least 1 hour for the flavours to blend.

3 Open out the lamb with skin side down. Season with salt and pepper, sprinkle with the thyme leaves and drizzle the honey over the top. Roll up and tie securely with string in several places. Place the meat in a roasting pan and put into the hot oven. Cook for 30 minutes until browned all over.

4 Pour the cider and 150ml/¼ pint/ ⅔ cup water into the tin. Lower the oven to 160°C/325°F/Gas 3 and cook for about 45 minutes for medium (pink) or about 1 hour for well done meat.

5 Remove the lamb from the oven, cover loosely with a sheet of foil and leave to stand for 20–30 minutes.

6 Lift the lamb on to a warmed serving plate. Skim any excess fat from the surface of the pan juices before reheating and seasoning to taste. Stir in the cream, if using, bring to the boil and remove from the heat. Carve the lamb and serve it with the pan juices spooned over and the mint sauce.

Energy 351kcal/1468kJ; Protein 36.9g; Carbohydrate 2.5g, of which sugars 2.5g; Fat 21g, of which saturates 9.8g; Cholesterol 143mg; Calcium 23mg; Fibre 0g; Sodium 202mg

Roast pork and apple sauce

Another traditional centrepiece for Sunday lunch with family or friends, a joint of roast pork is often eaten with apple sauce. Since Roman times it has been customary to offset the richness of the pork with sharp fruit flavours.

Serves 6

15ml/1 tbsp light olive oil

2 leeks, chopped

150g/5oz/⅔ cup ready-to-eat dried apricots, chopped

150g/5oz/1 cup dried dates, stoned (pitted) and chopped

75g/3oz/1½ cups fresh white breadcrumbs

2 eggs, beaten

15ml/1 tbsp fresh thyme leaves

1.5kg/3¼lb boned loin of pork

salt and ground black pepper

For the apple sauce

450g/1lb cooking apples

30ml/2 tbsp cider or water

25g/1oz/2 tbsp butter

about 25g/1oz/2 tbsp caster (superfine) sugar

1 Preheat the oven to 220°C/425°F/ Gas 7. To make the stuffing, heat the oil in a large pan and cook the leeks until softened. Remove from the heat and stir in the apricots, dates, breadcrumbs, eggs and thyme and season with salt and pepper.

2 Lay the pork skin side up, and use a very sharp knife to score the rind into diamonds. (You may find it easier to do this with a clean craft knife or scalpel.)

3 Turn the joint over and cut vertically down the centre of the meat to within 1cm/½in of the rind and fat, then cut horizontally from the middle outwards towards each side to open out the joint for stuffing.

4 Spoon half the stuffing into the cut surfaces, then fold the meat over. Tie the joint back into its original shape, then place in a roasting pan and rub the skin liberally with salt.

5 Put the joint into the hot oven and cook for 40 minutes. Reduce the temperature to 190°C/375°F/Gas 5 and cook for a further 1½ hours, or until the meat is cooked through – the juices should run clear when the meat is pierced with a sharp knife.

6 Meanwhile, shape the remaining stuffing into walnut-sized balls. Arrange on a tray, cover with clear film (plastic wrap) and chill until 30 minutes before the pork is cooked. Then add the balls to the roasting pan and baste them with the cooking juices from the meat.

7 To make the apple sauce, peel, core and chop the apples, then place in a small pan with the cider or water and cook, stirring occasionally, for 5–10 minutes, or until very soft. Beat well or blend in a blender or food processor until smooth. Beat in the butter and sugar to taste. Reheat the apple sauce just before serving, if necessary.

8 When the meat is cooked, cover it closely with foil and leave to stand in a warm place for 10 minutes to rest before carving. Carve the pork into thick slices and serve with pieces of the crackling, the stuffing balls and the apple sauce.

Energy 582kcal/2452kJ; Protein 59.9g; Carbohydrate 48.3g, of which sugars 38.6g; Fat 17.9g, of which saturates 6.5g; Cholesterol 230mg; Calcium 91mg; Fibre 5.2g; Sodium 327mg

Somerset cider-glazed ham

William the Conqueror is credited with bringing the art of cider-making to England from Normandy in 1066. This wonderful West Country ham glazed with cider is traditionally served with cranberry sauce and is ideal for a Sunday lunch with lots of guests.

Serves 8–10

2kg/4½lb middle gammon (smoked or cured ham) joint

2 small onions

about 30 whole cloves

3 bay leaves

10 black peppercorns

1.3 litres/2¼ pints/5⅔ cups medium-dry (hard) cider

45ml/3 tbsp soft light brown sugar

For the cranberry sauce

350g/12oz/3 cups cranberries

175g/6oz/¾ cup light brown sugar

grated rind and juice of 2 clementines

30ml/2 tbsp port

1 Weigh the ham and calculate the cooking time at 20 minutes per 450g/1lb, then place it in a large pan. Stud the onions with 5–10 cloves and add to the pan together with the bay leaves and peppercorns.

2 Add 1.2 litres/2 pints/5 cups of the cider and enough water just to cover the ham. Heat until simmering and skim off the scum that rises to the surface.

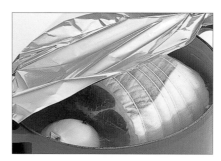

3 Start timing the cooking from the moment the stock begins to simmer. Cover with a lid or foil and simmer gently for the calculated time. Towards the end of the cooking time, preheat the oven to 220°C/425°F/Gas 7.

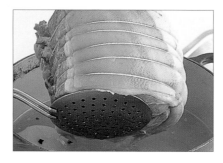

4 Lift the ham out of the pan. Leave to stand until cool enough to handle.

5 Heat the sugar and remaining cider in a pan until the sugar dissolves. Bubble gently for about 5 minutes to make a dark glaze. Remove the pan from the heat and leave to cool for 5 minutes.

6 Carefully and evenly, cut off the rind of the ham, then score the fat to make a neat diamond pattern. Place the ham in a roasting tin. Press a clove into the centre of each diamond, then carefully spoon the glaze over. Put into the hot oven and cook for 20–25 minutes, or until brown, glistening and crisp.

7 To make the cranberry sauce, simmer all the ingredients in a heavy pan for 15–20 minutes, stirring frequently, until the fruit bursts and the sauce thickens. Pour into a serving dish.

8 Serve the ham hot or cold with the cranberry sauce.

Cook's tips If the ham is likely to be very salty, soak it overnight in cold water to remove excess salt before cooking. Your butcher will advise you.
• Reserve the stock used to cook the ham and use it to make a hearty split pea or lentil soup.

Energy 368kcal/1541kJ; Protein 39.6g; Carbohydrate 15.2g, of which sugars 15.2g; Fat 16.9g, of which saturates 5.6g; Cholesterol 52mg; Calcium 25mg; Fibre 0.6g; Sodium 1982mg

Stuffed roast chicken with bread sauce

Chicken today is a popular choice for roasting. Free-range and organic birds taste best and are more like the birds that previous generations regarded as a luxury food. Roast sausages and potatoes with the bird for a proper Sunday lunch.

Serves 6

1 chicken weighing about 1.8kg/4lb, with giblets and neck if possible

1 small onion, sliced

1 small carrot, sliced

small bunch of parsley and thyme

15g/½oz/1 tbsp butter

30ml/2 tbsp oil

6 rashers (strips) fatty bacon

15ml/1 tbsp plain (all-purpose) flour

300ml/½ pint/1¼ cups chicken stock

salt and ground black pepper

For the stuffing

1 onion, finely chopped

50g/2oz/4 tbsp butter

150g/5oz/2½ cups fresh white breadcrumbs

15ml/1 tbsp chopped fresh parsley

15ml/1 tbsp chopped fresh herbs, such as thyme, marjoram and chives

grated rind and juice of ½ lemon

For the bread sauce

1 small onion, sliced

1 bay leaf

6 black peppercorns

2 whole cloves

pinch of mace or grated nutmeg

400ml/14fl oz/1⅔ cups milk

50g/2oz/1 cup fresh breadcrumbs

25g/1oz/2 tbsp butter.

1 Put the giblets and neck into a pan with the sliced onion and carrot and the bunch of parsley and thyme. Season with salt and pepper. Cover generously with cold water, bring to the boil and simmer gently for about 1 hour. Strain the stock, discarding the giblets. Preheat the oven to 200°C/400°F/Gas 6.

2 To make the stuffing, cook the onion in the butter in a large pan over low heat until soft. Remove from the heat and stir in the breadcrumbs, herbs, lemon rind and juice, salt and pepper.

3 Spoon the stuffing into the neck cavity of the chicken and secure the opening with a small skewer. Weigh the stuffed chicken and calculate the cooking time at 20 minutes per 450g/1lb plus 20 minutes extra. Spread the chicken breast with the butter, then put the oil into a roasting pan and sit the bird in it. Season and lay the bacon rashers over the breast.

4 Put the chicken into the hot oven. After 20 minutes, reduce the temperature to 180°C/350°F/Gas 4 and cook for the remaining time. To check the chicken is cooked, insert a sharp knife between the body and the thigh: if the juices run clear with no hint of blood, it is done.

5 Meanwhile, make the bread sauce. Into a pan, put the onion, bay leaf, peppercorns, cloves, mace and milk. Bring slowly to the boil, remove from the heat, cover and leave to stand for 30 minutes or longer to infuse. Strain and return the milk to the cleaned pan, add the breadcrumbs and seasoning. Heat until bubbling and simmer gently for about 10 minutes until thick and creamy. Stir in the butter and it is ready to serve.

6 Transfer the cooked chicken to a serving dish and allow it to rest for 10 minutes in a warm place while you make the gravy.

7 To make the gravy, pour off the excess fat from the roasting pan, then sprinkle in the flour. Cook gently, stirring, for 1–2 minutes. Gradually add the stock, scraping the pan to lift the residue and stirring well until smooth. Bring to the boil, stirring and adding extra stock if necessary. Adjust the seasoning to taste.

8 Carve the chicken, and serve with the gravy and bread sauce.

Cook's tip If you prefer not to stuff the chicken, the stuffing can be formed into small balls and baked around the bird for the last 20–30 minutes of the cooking time.

Energy 823kcal/3420kJ; Protein 55.7g; Carbohydrate 21.1g, of which sugars 19.1g; Fat 57.8g, of which saturates 19.7g; Cholesterol 383mg; Calcium 113mg; Fibre 4.9g; Sodium 252mg

Chicken with lemon and herbs

If you don't have time to cook a roast, or just cooking for two but still want chicken for Sunday lunch, combine the rich flavour of chicken thigh meat with tangy citrus and fresh herbs, and you have a dish that will be popular at any time of year.

Serves 2

50g/2oz/4 tbsp butter

2 spring onions (scallions), white part only, finely chopped

15ml/1 tbsp chopped fresh tarragon

15ml/1 tbsp chopped fresh dill

juice of 1 lemon

4 chicken thighs

salt and ground black pepper

lemon slices and herb sprigs, to garnish

1 Preheat the grill (broiler) to medium. In a small pan, heat the butter gently until melted, then remove from the heat and add the chopped spring onions, tarragon, dill and lemon juice. Season with salt and pepper.

2 Brush the chicken with the herb mixture. Grill (broil) for 10–12 minutes, basting frequently. Turn over and baste again, then cook for a further 10–12 minutes or until the juices run clear. Garnish with lemon slices and herbs.

Energy 406kcal/1692kJ; Protein 42.1g; Carbohydrate 0.5g, of which sugars 0.4g; Fat 26.2g, of which saturates 14.7g; Cholesterol 263mg; Calcium 22mg; Fibre 0.3g; Sodium 333mg

Chicken with red cabbage

Red cabbage is not just for pickling, though that seems to be the only way it was eaten in England until the late 20th century. Teamed with chicken and braised, it makes a delicious autumn or winter Sunday lunch. Cooked chestnuts are available vacuum packed or frozen.

Serves 4

50g/2oz/4 tbsp butter

4 chicken thighs

4 chicken drumsticks

1 onion, chopped

500g/1¼lb red cabbage, finely shredded

4 juniper berries, crushed

12 peeled, cooked chestnuts

125ml/4fl oz/½ cup red wine

salt and ground black pepper

1 Heat the butter in a heavy flameproof casserole and lightly brown the chicken pieces. Lift out. Add the onion to the casserole and cook gently until soft and golden. Stir in the cabbage and juniper berries, season and cook for 6–7 minutes, stirring once or twice.

2 Add the chestnuts, then tuck the chicken under the cabbage on the bottom of the casserole. Add the wine.

3 Cover and cook gently for 40 minutes until the cabbage is very tender. Adjust the seasoning to taste.

Energy 405kcal/1697kJ; Protein 44.9g; Carbohydrate 18.6g, of which sugars 9.2g; Fat 14.9g, of which saturates 7.7g; Cholesterol 189mg; Calcium 94mg; Fibre 4.1g; Sodium 229mg

Roast goose with apples

The goose goes far back into the culinary history of England. Today it is a seasonal and costly treat that is popular at Christmas and New Year, but it was traditionally served on Michaelmas Day (29 September), having been fattened on barley stubble after the harvest, and it was said to bring financial luck to those who ate it then. Apples are in season at the same time and their fresh sharp flavour offsets the richness of the goose beautifully.

Serves 8

1 oven-ready goose weighing about 5.5kg/12lb, with giblets

1 small onion, sliced

2 small carrots, sliced

2 celery sticks, sliced

small bunch of parsley and thyme

450/1lb black pudding (blood sausage), crumbled or chopped

1 large garlic clove, crushed

2 large cooking apples, peeled, cored and finely chopped

250ml/8fl oz/1 cup dry (hard) cider

about 15ml/1 tbsp flour

salt and ground black pepper

roast potatoes and freshly cooked seasonal vegetables, to serve

1 Remove the goose liver from the giblets and put the the rest of the giblets into a pan with the onion, carrots, celery and herbs. Cover with cold water, season and simmer for 30–45 minutes to make a stock for the gravy, top up with water if necessary. Preheat the oven to 200°C/400°F/Gas 6

Cook's tips When buying a goose, allow about 675g/1½lb per person.
• Save the copious fat that you drain from the goose during cooking and store in the refrigerator. It keeps for several weeks, and you can use it to roast the crispest, most delicious potatoes and parsnips for future meals.

2 Meanwhile, chop the liver finely and mix it with the black pudding, garlic and apples. Add salt and black pepper to the stuffing, then sprinkle in 75ml/2½fl oz/⅓ cup cider to bind it.

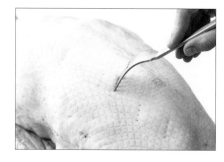

3 Wipe out the goose and stuff it with this mixture. Prick the skin all over with a fork, sprinkle generously with salt and pepper and rub in well.

4 Weigh the stuffed goose and calculate the correct cooking time at 15 minutes per 450g/1lb and 15 minutes over. Put the goose on a rack in a large roasting pan, cover with foil and put it into the preheated oven.

5 After 1 hour, remove the goose from the oven and carefully pour off the hot fat that has accumulated. Pour the remaining dry cider over the goose, replace the foil, and return to the oven.

6 Half an hour before the end of the estimated cooking time, remove the foil and baste the goose with the juices. Return to the oven, uncovered, and allow the skin to brown and crisp.

7 The goose is cooked if the juices run clear when the thickest part of the thigh is pierced with a skewer. Transfer the goose to a warmed serving plate, and rest in a warm place for at least 20 minutes before carving.

8 While the goose is resting, make the gravy. Pour off any excess fat from the roasting pan, leaving 30ml/2 tbsp, then sprinkle in enough flour to absorb it.

9 Cook over a medium heat for 1 minute, scraping the pan to loosen the sediment. Strain the giblet stock and stir in enough to make the gravy.

10 Bring the gravy to the boil and simmer for a few minutes, stirring constantly. Add any juices that have accumulated under the cooked goose, season to taste and pour the gravy into a heated sauceboat.

11 Carve the goose into slices at the table and serve with the gravy, roast potatoes and some seasonal vegetables.

Energy 822kcal/3437kJ; Protein 54.8g; Carbohydrate 44.1g, of which sugars 21.8g; Fat 48.7g, of which saturates 0.9g; Cholesterol 0mg; Calcium 87mg; Fibre 3.1g; Sodium 486mg

Duck with plum sauce

This is an updated version of an old English dish that was traditionally served in the late summer and early autumn, when Victoria plums are ripe and abundant. The sharp, fruity flavour of the plums balances the richness of the duck.

Serves 4

4 duck quarters

1 large red onion, finely chopped

500g/1¼lb ripe plums, quartered and stoned (pitted)

30ml/2 tbsp redcurrant jelly

salt and ground black pepper

1 Prick the duck skin all over with a fork to release the fat during cooking and help give a crisp result, then place the portions in a heavy frying pan, skin side down.

Cook's tip Make sure the plums are very ripe, otherwise the mixture may be too dry and the sauce extremely tart.

2 Cook the duck pieces for 10 minutes on each side, or until golden brown and cooked right through. Remove the duck from the frying pan, using tongs or a draining spoon, and keep warm.

Variations The red onion can be replaced with a white or a brown one.
• Fine cut orange marmalade makes a tangy alternative to the redcurrant jelly.

3 Pour away all but 30ml/2 tbsp of the duck fat, then stir-fry the onion for 5 minutes, or until golden. Add the plums and cook for a further 5 minutes, stirring. Add the redcurrant jelly.

4 Replace the duck portions and cook for a further 5 minutes or until thoroughly reheated. Season with salt and pepper to taste before serving.

Energy 608kcal/2515kJ; Protein 15.1g; Carbohydrate 17.4g, of which sugars 17g; Fat 53.5g, of which saturates 14.5g; Cholesterol 0mg; Calcium 35mg; Fibre 2.2g; Sodium 102mg

Pheasant with mushrooms, chestnuts and bacon

Braising is a slow, gentle cooking method, ideal for pheasants available at the end of the season, when they are no longer tender enough to roast but are full of flavour. Here they are cooked with mushrooms and chestnuts, which are in season at the same time.

Serves 4

2 mature pheasants

50g/2oz/4 tbsp butter

75ml/5 tbsp brandy

12 baby (pearl) onions, peeled

1 celery stick, chopped

50g/2oz unsmoked rindless bacon

45ml/3 tbsp plain (all-purpose) flour

550ml/18fl oz/2½ cups chicken stock

175g/6oz peeled, cooked chestnuts

350g/12oz/4 cups mixed wild mushrooms, trimmed and sliced

15ml/1 tbsp lemon juice

salt and ground black pepper

1 Preheat the oven to 160°C/325°F/Gas 3. Season the pheasants with salt and pepper. Melt half the butter in a large flameproof casserole and brown on all sides over a medium heat. Transfer them to a shallow roasting dish.

2 Pour off the excess fat from the casserole and return it to the heat. Add the brandy, stir to loosen the sediment, then pour over the pheasants.

3 Wipe out the casserole and melt the remaining butter. Cut the bacon into strips and brown in the butter with the onions and celery for 5 minutes. Sprinkle the flour into the casserole and cook, stirring, for 1 minute.

4 Gradually add the chicken stock, stirring until smooth. Add the chestnuts, mushrooms, the pheasants and their juices and bring back to a gentle simmer. Cover the dish, put into the hot oven and cook for 1½ hours or until the pheasants are tender.

5 Bring the sauce back to the boil, add the lemon juice and season to taste. Transfer the cooked pheasants and vegetables to a warmed serving plate. Pour over some of the sauce and serve the rest on the side.

Energy 883kcal/3699kJ; Protein 86.8g; Carbohydrate 32.3g, of which sugars 6.9g; Fat 41.6g, of which saturates 15.8g; Cholesterol 35mg; Calcium 205mg; Fibre 2.9g; Sodium 920mg

Roast pheasant with game chips

The game season begins on 1 October, when hen pheasants are in their prime, so this is an autumnal Sunday dish. The addition of bacon, covering the breast, helps to keep the moisture in the roasted meat. Crisp-fried game chips are the traditional accompaniment.

Serves 2

1 hen pheasant

25g/1oz/2 tbsp butter

115g/4oz rindless streaky (fatty) bacon rashers (strips)

2 medium potatoes

oil, for deep-frying

salt and ground black pepper

For the stuffing

25g/1oz/2 tbsp butter

1 leek, chopped

115g/4oz peeled, cooked chestnuts, coarsely chopped (see Cook's tip)

30ml/2 tbsp chopped fresh flat-leaf parsley

For the gravy

15ml/1 tbsp cornflour (cornstarch)

300ml/½ pint/1¼ cups well-flavoured chicken stock

50ml/2fl oz/¼ cup port

1 Preheat the oven to 190°C/375°F/ Gas 5. Pick any stray quills or stubs of feathers from the pheasant and season the bird inside and out with salt and black pepper.

Cook's tip For convenience, use vacuum-packed or frozen chestnuts rather than fresh, which are fiddly to peel and cook. Simply rinse the chestnuts thoroughly with boiling water and drain before using. Whole, unsweetened canned chestnuts could be used, but they tend to be fairly dense and can be soft.

2 Carefully loosen and lift the skin covering the breast and rub the butter between the skin and flesh.

3 To make the stuffing, melt the butter in a pan and cook the leek for about 5 minutes until softened but not coloured. Remove from the heat and mix in the chopped chestnuts, parsley and seasoning to taste.

4 Spoon the stuffing into the cavity of the pheasant and secure the opening with skewers. Arrange the bacon over the breast and place in a roasting pan.

5 Put into the hot oven and cook for 1–1½ hours, or until the juices run clear when the bird is pierced with a skewer in the thickest part of the leg.

6 Lift out and cover closely with foil, then leave to stand in a warm place for 15 minutes before carving.

7 On the stove, heat the juices in the roasting pan and stir in the cornflour. Gradually stir in the stock and port. Bring to the boil, then reduce the heat and simmer for about 5 minutes, until the sauce is slightly thickened and glossy. Strain the sauce and keep warm.

8 Peel the potatoes and cut into matchsticks. Heat the oil in a deep-fat fryer or large pan to 190°C/375°F and fry the chips until crisp, golden and cooked through. Drain on kitchen paper.

9 Serve the pheasant with the gravy and game chips.

Energy 897kcal/3742kJ; Protein 70.6g; Carbohydrate 34.3g, of which sugars 9.1g; Fat 50.8g, of which saturates 20g; Cholesterol 524mg; Calcium 127mg; Fibre 4.5g; Sodium 946mg

Steak and oyster pie

In the 17th century, oysters were so plentiful and cheap that not only could the poor afford to eat them, they were even used to feed animals. When enormous beef pies were prepared for large gatherings, oysters were added to make the beef go further. Though oysters are a luxury today, they make this pie into a real Sunday treat.

Serves 6

30ml/2 tbsp plain (all-purpose) flour

1kg/2¼lb rump (round) steak, cut into 5cm/2in pieces

45ml/3 tbsp oil

25g/1oz/2 tbsp butter

1 large onion, chopped

300ml/½ pint/1¼ cups beef stock

300ml/½ pint/1¼ cups brown ale or red wine

30ml/2 tbsp fresh thyme leaves

225g/8oz chestnut mushrooms, halved if large

12 shelled oysters

375g/13oz puff pastry, thawed if frozen

salt and ground black pepper

beaten egg, to glaze

1 Preheat the oven if using (see step 3) to 150°C/300°F/Gas 2. Season the flour with salt and pepper and toss the pieces of steak in it until well coated. Heat half the oil with half the butter in a large pan or flameproof casserole and quickly brown the meat in batches. Set the steak aside.

2 Add the remaining oil and butter to the hot pan, stir in the chopped onion and cook over a medium heat, stirring occasionally, until golden brown and beginning to soften.

3 Return the meat and any juices to the pan and stir in the stock, ale or wine and thyme. Bring just to the boil then cover the pan and either simmer very gently on the stove or cook in the preheated oven for about 1½ hours, or until the beef is tender.

4 Using a slotted spoon, lift the meat and onion out of the liquid and put it into a 1.75 litre/3 pint/7½ cup pie dish. Bring the liquid to the boil and reduce to about 600ml/1 pint/2½ cups.

Cook's tip Though using rump steak for the pie is traditional, replacing it with the same amount of braising steak is acceptable.

5 Season to taste and stir in the mushrooms, then pour the mixture over the meat in the dish. Leave to cool. Preheat the oven to 200°C/400°F/Gas 6, if not already using.

6 Add the oysters to the cooled meat, pushing them down into the mixture.

7 Roll out the pastry on a lightly floured surface to a shape 2.5cm/1in larger than the dish. Trim off a 1cm/½in strip all around the edge. Brush the rim of the dish with a little beaten egg and lay the strip on it. Brush the strip with egg, lay the pastry sheet over the top, trim to fit and press the edges together well to seal them. Brush the top of the pie with beaten egg.

8 Put the pie into the hot oven and cook for about 40 minutes, until the pastry is crisp and golden brown and the filling is piping hot.

Energy 689kcal/2874kJ; Protein 49.4g; Carbohydrate 29.8g, of which sugars 1g; Fat 39g, of which saturates 9.1g; Cholesterol 144mg; Calcium 145mg; Fibre 0.4g; Sodium 674mg

Beef Wellington

This dish is derived from the classic French *boeuf en croûte*. The English name was applied to it in honour of the Duke of Wellington, following his victory at the Battle of Waterloo in 1815. It is traditionally served at dinner, but is also perfect for Sunday lunch. Begin the dish well in advance to allow time for the meat to cool before it is wrapped in pastry.

Serves 6

1.5kg/3lb 6oz fillet of beef

45ml/3 tbsp oil

115g/4oz mushrooms, chopped

2 garlic cloves, crushed

175g/6oz smooth liver pâté

30ml/2 tbsp chopped fresh parsley

400g/14oz puff pastry

salt and ground black pepper

beaten egg, to glaze

1 Tie the fillet at intervals with string. Heat 30ml/2 tbsp of the oil, and brown on all sides over a high heat. Transfer to a roasting tin and cook in the oven for 20 minutes. Leave to cool.

2 Heat the remaining oil and cook the mushrooms and garlic for 5 minutes. Beat the mushrooms into the pâté. Add the parsley, season and leave to cool.

3 Roll out the pastry, reserving a small amount, into a rectangle large enough to enclose the beef. Spread the pâté mixture down the middle, untie the beef and lay it on the pâté.

4 Preheat the oven to 220°C/425°F/ Gas 7. Brush the pastry edges with beaten egg and fold it over the meat. Place, seam down, on a baking sheet. Cut leaves from the reserved pastry and decorate the top. Brush the parcel with beaten egg. Chill for 10 minutes or until the oven is hot.

5 Cook for 50–60 minutes, covering loosely with foil after about 30 minutes to prevent the pastry burning. Cut into thick slices to serve.

Energy 511kcal/2131kJ; Protein 41.7g; Carbohydrate 19.3g, of which sugars 1.2g; Fat 30.6g, of which saturates 7.2g; Cholesterol 128mg; Calcium 41mg; Fibre 0.4g; Sodium 320mg

Chicken and leek pies

This is a traditional English pie that makes a lovely main course for a Sunday lunch. You can also make individual pies in small tart tins or a four-hole Yorkshire pudding tin. Serve the pie with roast potatoes and braised carrots, and finish off the meal with a non-pastry dessert.

Serves 4

400g/14oz shortcrust pastry, thawed if frozen

15g/½oz/1 tbsp butter

1 leek, thinly sliced

2 eggs

225g/8oz skinless chicken breast fillets, finely chopped

small handful of fresh parsley or mint, finely chopped

salt and ground black pepper

beaten egg, to glaze

1 Preheat the oven to 200°C/400°F/ Gas 6. Roll out the pastry on a lightly floured surface to a thickness of about 3mm/⅛in. Cut out two circles, each large enough to fit a 20cm/8in tin or pie plate. Use one circle to line line the base of the tin. Set the other circle aside to make the lid.

2 To make the filling, melt the butter in a pan, add the leek and cook gently for about 5 minutes, stirring occasionally, until soft but not brown.

Variation
The pie is just as nice made with puff pastry instead of shortcrust.

3 Beat the eggs in a bowl and stir in the chicken, herbs and seasoning. Add the leek and its buttery juices from the pan, stirring until well mixed.

4 Spoon the mixture into the pastry case, filling it generously. Brush the edges of the pastry with beaten egg and place the lid on top, trimming the excess with a sharp knife and pressing the edges together to seal. Brush the tops of the pie with beaten egg and make a small slit in the centre to allow steam to escape.

5 Put into the hot oven and cook for about 30 minutes, until golden brown and cooked through.

Energy 588kcal/2459kJ; Protein 23.4g; Carbohydrate 48.4g, of which sugars 2.1g; Fat 34.9g, of which saturates 11.7g; Cholesterol 157mg; Calcium 133mg; Fibre 3.4g; Sodium 496mg

Veal and ham pie

In the cold version of veal and ham pie, the filling is completely enclosed in hot water crust pastry. In this hot version, the pastry sits on top of the classic combination of meat and eggs, keeping the contents moist and the aromas sealed in until the pie is cut open.

Serves 4

450g/1lb boneless shoulder of veal, cut into cubes

225g/8oz lean gammon, cut into cubes

15ml/1 tbsp plain (all-purpose) flour

large pinch each of dry mustard and ground black pepper

25g/1oz/2 tbsp butter

15ml/1 tbsp oil

1 onion, chopped

600ml/1 pint/2½ cups chicken or veal stock

2 eggs, hard-boiled and sliced

30ml/2 tbsp chopped fresh parsley

For the pastry

175g/6oz/1½ cups plain (all-purpose) flour

pinch of salt

85g/3oz/6 tbsp butter, diced

beaten egg, to glaze

1 Preheat the oven to 180°C/350°F/Gas 4. Mix the veal and gammon in a bowl. Season the flour with the mustard and black pepper, then add it to the meat and toss well.

2 Heat the butter and oil in a large, flameproof casserole until sizzling, then cook the meat mixture in batches until golden on all sides. Use a slotted spoon to remove the meat and set aside.

3 Cook the onion in the fat remaining in the casserole until softened but not coloured. Stir in the stock and the meat. Cover and cook in the hot oven for 1½ hours or until the veal is tender. Adjust the seasoning and leave to cool.

4 To make the pastry, sift the flour into a bowl with the salt and rub in the butter until the mixture resembles fine crumbs. Mix in just enough cold water to bind the mixture, gathering it together with your fingertips. Wrap the pastry in clear film (plastic wrap), and chill for at least 30 minutes.

Variation Use ready-made fresh or frozen puff pastry to cover the pie.

5 Spoon the veal mixture into a 1.5 litre/2½ pint/6¼ cup pie dish. Arrange the slices of hard-boiled egg on top and sprinkle with the parsley.

6 On a lightly floured surface, roll out the pastry to about 4cm/1½in larger than the top of the pie dish. Cut a strip from around the edge, dampen the rim of the dish and press the pastry strip on to it. Brush the pastry rim with beaten egg and top with the lid.

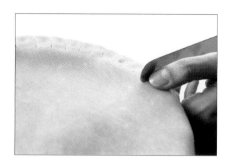

7 Trim off any excess pastry. Use the blunt edge of a knife to tap the outside edge, pressing the pastry down with your finger to seal in the filling. Pinch the pastry between your fingers to flute the edge. Roll out any trimmings and cut out shapes to decorate the pie.

8 Brush the top of the pie with beaten egg, put into the hot oven and cook for 30–40 minutes or until the pastry is well risen and golden brown. Serve hot.

Energy 621kcal/2595kJ; Protein 42.4g; Carbohydrate 39.2g, of which sugars 2.6g; Fat 33.8g, of which saturates 17.2g; Cholesterol 281mg; Calcium 128mg; Fibre 2.3g; Sodium 1007mg

Cheese and asparagus flan

The English asparagus season is short, so make a summer Sunday lunch that makes the most of this distinctive vegetable. The taste of fresh asparagus comes through beautifully in this flan, and, as it has an affinity with cheese, each ingredient enhances the flavour of the other.

Serves 5–6

175g/6oz/1½ cups plain (all-purpose) flour

pinch of salt

40g/1½oz/3 tbsp lard, diced

40g/1½oz/3 tbsp butter, diced

300g/11oz small asparagus spears weighed after trimming

75g/3oz mature Cheddar cheese, grated

3 spring onions (scallions), thinly sliced

2 eggs

300ml/½ pint/1¼ cups double (heavy) cream

freshly grated nutmeg

salt and ground black pepper

1 To make the pastry, sift the flour and salt into a bowl and add the lard and butter. With your fingertips, rub the fats into the flour until the mixture resembles fine breadcrumbs.

2 Stir in about 45ml/3 tbsp cold water until the mixture can be gathered together into a ball of dough. (Or use a food processor.) Wrap the pastry and chill for 30 minutes.

3 Put a flat baking sheet in the oven and preheat to 200°C/400°F/Gas 6. Roll out the pastry on a lightly floured work surface and use it to line a 20cm/8in flan tin (pan).

4 Line the pastry case (pie shell) with baking parchment or foil and add a layer of baking beans. Put the flan tin on to the heated baking sheet in the oven and cook for 10–15 minutes until set. Carefully remove the beans and parchment or foil, return the pastry to the oven and cook for a further 5 minutes, until light golden brown on the edges. Remove the flan and reduce the temperature to 180°C/350°F/Gas 4.

5 Meanwhile, cook the asparagus spears in lightly salted boiling water for 2–3 minutes or until only just tender. Drain, rinse under cold water and dry on kitchen paper. Cut the asparagus spears into 2.5cm/1in lengths, leaving the tips whole.

6 Scatter half the cheese in the base of the cooked pastry case and add the asparagus and the spring onions.

7 Beat the eggs with the cream and season with salt, pepper and nutmeg.

8 Pour over the asparagus and top with the remaining cheese.

9 Return the flan to the hot baking sheet in the oven and cook for about 30 minutes or until just set. Leave the flan to settle for 5 minutes before cutting and serving.

Energy 547kcal/2266kJ; Protein 10.4g; Carbohydrate 24.7g, of which sugars 2.4g; Fat 45.6g, of which saturates 26.2g; Cholesterol 165mg; Calcium 184mg; Fibre 1.8g; Sodium 167mg

Asparagus with hollandaise sauce

Since the 16th century England has produced this "queen of vegetables", at its finest for a short season in early summer. Serve it simply – drizzled with melted unsalted butter, or with hollandaise sauce, as an accompaniment to poached fish or roasted chicken.

Serves 4

2 bunches of asparagus

30ml/2 tbsp white wine vinegar

2 egg yolks

115g/4oz butter, melted

juice of ½ lemon

salt and ground black pepper

Cook's tips Asparagus should be cooked and eaten as soon as possible, preferably on the day it is picked.
• Asparagus is also good served cold with mayonnaise.
• Make stock with the woody ends of the asparagus rather throwing them away and add it to vegetable soups or sauces.

1 Snap off the tough ends of the asparagus. Drop the spears into fast boiling water, cooking for 1–2 minutes until just tender. Test the thickest part of the stalk with a small sharp knife; take care not to overcook.

2 In a pan, bring the vinegar to the boil and bubble until it has reduced to just 15ml/1 tbsp. Remove from the heat and add 15ml/1 tbsp cold water.

3 Whisk the egg yolks into the vinegar and water mixture, then put the pan over a very low heat and continue whisking until the mixture is frothy and thickened.

4 Remove from the heat again and slowly whisk in the melted butter. Add the lemon juice and seasoning to taste. Serve the sauce immediately with the drained asparagus.

Energy 276kcal/1135kJ; Protein 5.3g; Carbohydrate 2.7g, of which sugars 2.6g; Fat 27.1g, of which saturates 15.9g; Cholesterol 162mg; Calcium 51mg; Fibre 2.1g; Sodium 180mg

Cauliflower cheese

This cheese sauce is French in origin but has become a staple of English cookery, and can also be used with carrots or broccoli. Cauliflower cheese goes perfectly with glazed ham, and roast lamb, and is also delicious with braised red cabbage and roast potatoes.

Serves 4

1 medium cauliflower

25g/1oz/2 tbsp butter

25g/1oz/4 tbsp plain (all-purpose) flour

300ml/½ pint/1¼ cups milk

115g/4oz mature Cheddar or Cheshire cheese, grated

salt and ground black pepper

1 Trim the cauliflower and cut it into florets. Bring a pan of lightly salted water to the boil, drop in the cauliflower and cook for 5–8 minutes or until just tender. Drain and tip the florets into an ovenproof dish.

2 To make the sauce, melt the butter in a pan, stir in the flour and cook gently, stirring constantly, for about 1 minute (do not allow it to brown). Remove from the heat and gradually stir in the milk. Return the pan to the heat and cook, stirring, until the mixture thickens and comes to the boil. Simmer gently for 1–2 minutes.

3 Stir in three-quarters of the cheese and season to taste. Spoon the sauce over the cauliflower and scatter the remaining cheese on top. Put under a hot grill (broiler) until golden brown.

Cook's tip Boost the cheese flavour by adding a little English (hot) mustard to the cheese sauce.

Energy 318kcal/1318kJ; Protein 17.4g; Carbohydrate 4.4g, of which sugars 3.9g; Fat 25.8g, of which saturates 16.3g; Cholesterol 71mg; Calcium 371mg; Fibre 1.8g; Sodium 453mg

Braised leeks with carrots

Sweet carrots and leeks go well together and are good finished with a little chopped mint, chervil or parsley. This is an excellent accompaniment to roast beef, lamb or chicken.

2 Uncover the pan and boil until the juices have evaporated, leaving the carrots moist and glazed. Remove from the pan and set aside.

3 Melt 25g/1oz/2 tbsp of the remaining butter in the pan. Add the leeks and cook over a low heat for 4–5 minutes, without allowing them to brown.

4 Add seasoning, a good pinch of sugar, the wine and half the chopped herbs. Heat until simmering, then cover and cook gently for 5–8 minutes, until the leeks are tender but not collapsed. Uncover and turn the leeks in the buttery juices, then increase the heat and boil the liquid rapidly until reduced to a few tablespoonfuls.

Serves 4

70g/2½oz/5 tbsp butter

675g/1½lb carrots, thickly sliced

2 fresh bay leaves

pinch of sugar

675g/1½lb leeks, cut into 5cm/2in lengths

125ml/4fl oz/½ cup white wine

30ml/2 tbsp chopped fresh mint, chervil or parsley

salt and ground black pepper

1 Melt 25g/1oz/2 tbsp of the butter in a wide, heavy pan and cook the carrots, without allowing them to brown, for about 5 minutes. Add the bay leaves, seasoning, a pinch of sugar and 75ml/5 tbsp water. Bring to the boil, cover and cook for 10 minutes, or until the carrots are just tender.

5 Add the carrots to the leeks and reheat gently, stirring occasionally, then add the remaining butter. Adjust the seasoning. Transfer to a warmed serving dish and serve sprinkled with the remaining chopped herbs.

Energy 163kcal/677kJ; Protein 3.8g; Carbohydrate 18.5g, of which sugars 16.4g; Fat 6.5g, of which saturates 3.6g; Cholesterol 13mg; Calcium 87mg; Fibre 7.8g; Sodium 85mg

Brussels sprouts with chestnuts

Native to southern Europe, chestnuts arrived in England with the Romans. The fresh nuts are available in early winter and are an indispensable feature of Christmas dinner.

Serves 6

350g/12oz fresh chestnuts

300ml/½ pint/1¼ cups chicken or vegetable stock (optional)

5ml/1 tsp sugar

675g/1½lb Brussels sprouts

50g/2oz/4 tbsp butter

115g/4oz bacon, cut into strips

1 Cut a cross in the pointed end of each chestnut, then cook in boiling water for 5–10 minutes.

2 Drain the chestnuts, then peel off both the tough outer skin and the fine inner one. Return the chestnuts to the pan, add the stock (if using) or water and sugar and simmer gently for 30–35 minutes, until the chestnuts are tender, then drain thoroughly.

3 Meanwhile, cook the sprouts in lightly salted boiling water for 8–10 minutes, until tender, then drain well.

4 Melt the butter, add the bacon, cook until becoming crisp, then stir in the chestnuts for 2–3 minutes. Add the hot sprouts, toss together and serve.

Braised celery

Use some of the celery leaves, chopped, to garnish, or save them for salads or for flavouring stocks. Serve this dish to accompany any roast meat or fish dish.

Serves 4

40g/1½oz/3 tbsp butter

2 bacon rashers, chopped

1 small onion, finely chopped

1 carrot, finely chopped

1 celery head, cut into short lengths

175ml/6fl oz/¾ cup chicken or vegetable stock

1 bay leaf

1 parsley sprig

salt and ground black pepper

1 Melt the butter in a large heavy pan, then cook the bacon, onion and carrot until beginning to colour.

2 Add the celery and cook over a medium heat for 2–3 minutes. Stir in the stock, bay leaf, parsley and seasoning and bring to the boil.

3 Cover and simmer gently for about 25 minutes, until the celery is tender and the liquid reduced to a few tablespoonfuls. Serve hot.

Energy 256kcal/1070kJ; Protein 8.3g; Carbohydrate 26g, of which sugars 7.6g; Fat 13.9g, of which saturates 6.6g; Cholesterol 30mg; Calcium 59mg; Fibre 7g; Sodium 364mg

Energy 120kcal/496kJ; Protein 3g; Carbohydrate 3.4g, of which sugars 3g; Fat 10.6g, of which saturates 6g; Cholesterol 28mg; Calcium 61mg; Fibre 1.9g; Sodium 332mg

Braised red cabbage

In the English culinary tradition red cabbage has usually been pickled. However, it is a robust winter vegetable that takes on a beautiful colour and texture when cooked slowly and gently. This spiced version goes particularly well with pork, duck or game.

Serves 4–6

1kg/2¼lb red cabbage

2 onions, chopped

2 cooking apples, peeled, cored and coarsely grated

5ml/1 tsp freshly grated nutmeg

1.5ml/¼ tsp ground cloves

1.5ml/¼ tsp ground cinnamon

15ml/1 tbsp dark brown sugar

45ml/3 tbsp cider vinegar

25g/1oz/2 tbsp butter, cut into small pieces

salt and ground black pepper

1 Preheat the oven to 160°C/325°F/ Gas 3. Remove the large white ribs from the outer cabbage leaves, then shred the cabbage finely.

Cook's tip The braised cabbage can be cooked in advance and reheated in the oven for 30 minutes when needed. Leftovers can also be frozen.

2 Layer the shredded cabbage in a large ovenproof dish with the onions, apples, spices, sugar and seasoning. Pour the vinegar over and dot with the butter.

3 Cover, put into the hot oven and cook for about 1½ hours, stirring a couple of times, until the cabbage is very tender. Serve hot.

Energy 74kcal/309kJ; Protein 2.1g; Carbohydrate 10.1g, of which sugars 9.5g; Fat 3g, of which saturates 0.4g; Cholesterol 0mg; Calcium 53mg; Fibre 3.1g; Sodium 38mg

Roast beetroot with horseradish cream

Beetroot was very popular in Elizabethan days, when its vibrant colour was added to elaborate salads. In this recipe, its sweet flavour is enhanced first by roasting and then by the horseradish and vinegar in the cream. Serve it with roast beef or venison.

Serves 4–6

10–12 small whole beetroot

30ml/2 tbsp oil

45ml/3 tbsp grated fresh horseradish

15ml/1 tbsp white wine vinegar

10ml/2 tsp caster (superfine) sugar

150ml/¼ pint/⅔ cup double (heavy) cream

salt

Cook's tips If you are unable to find any fresh horseradish root use preserved grated horseradish instead.
• For a lighter sauce, replace half the cream with thick plain yogurt.

1 Preheat the oven to 180°C/350°F/ Gas 4. Wash the beetroot without breaking their skins. Trim the stalks very short but do not remove them completely. Toss the beetroot in the oil and sprinkle with salt. Spread them in a roasting pan and cover with foil. Put into the hot oven and cook for about 1½ hours or until soft throughout. Leave to cool, covered, for 10 minutes.

2 Meanwhile, make the horseradish sauce. Put the horseradish, vinegar and sugar into a bowl and mix well. Whip the cream until thickened and fold in the horseradish mixture. Cover and chill until required.

3 When the beetroot are cool enough to handle, slip off the skins and serve with the sauce.

Energy 254kcal/1052kJ; Protein 2.1g; Carbohydrate 10g, of which sugars 9.1g; Fat 22.2g, of which saturates 3.2g; Cholesterol 1mg; Calcium 26mg; Fibre 2.3g; Sodium 143mg

Roast parsnips with honey and nutmeg

The Romans considered parsnips to be a luxury, at which time they were credited with a variety of medicinal and aphrodisiac qualities. Today, they are especially enjoyed when roasted around a joint of beef, but they enhance any Sunday main course.

Serves 4–6

4 medium parsnips

30ml/2 tbsp plain (all-purpose) flour seasoned with salt and pepper

60ml/4 tbsp oil

15–30ml/1–2 tbsp clear honey

freshly grated nutmeg

1 Preheat the oven to 200°C/400°F/ Gas 6. Peel the parsnips and cut each one lengthways into quarters, removing any woody cores. Drop into a pan of boiling water and cook for 5 minutes until slightly softened.

2 Drain the parsnips thoroughly, then toss in the seasoned flour, shaking off any excess.

3 Pour the oil into a roasting pan and put into the oven until hot. Add the parsnips, tossing them in the oil and arranging them in a single layer.

4 Return the pan to the oven and cook the parsnips for about 30 minutes, turning occasionally, until crisp, golden brown and cooked through.

5 Drizzle with the honey and sprinkle a little grated nutmeg. Return the parsnips to the oven for 5 minutes before serving.

Parsnip chips

Before sugar was available, parsnips were used to sweeten cakes and jams. By the 20th century they had become an everyday item and were even dried to make "coffee" during World War II. These chips are particularly good served with roast chicken or sausages.

Serves 4

oil, for deep frying

2 large parsnips

30ml/2 tbsp plain (all-purpose) flour

salt

good pinch of curry powder (optional)

Variation For thicker chips, cut the parsnips lengthwise into wedges, removing any woody core, and boil until almost tender, then flour them and deep-fry.

1 Heat the oil to about 180°C/350°F. Season the flour with salt and curry powder, if using.

2 Peel the parsnips and, using a potato peeler, cut lengthways into thin strips. Put them into a pan, cover with water and bring just to the boil. Drain and dry thoroughly, then toss the strips in the seasoned flour.

3 Fry the strips, in batches, in the hot oil until crisp and golden brown outside and soft inside. Lift out and drain on kitchen paper. Sprinkle with a little salt and curry powder (if using) to serve.

Energy 144kcal/600kJ; Protein 2g; Carbohydrate 16.2g, of which sugars 6.7g; Fat 8.3g, of which saturates 1g; Cholesterol 0mg; Calcium 41mg; Fibre 4g; Sodium 9mg

Energy 230kcal/956kJ; Protein 2.3g; Carbohydrate 16.8g, of which sugars 5.1g; Fat 17.6g, of which saturates 2.1g; Cholesterol 0mg; Calcium 47mg; Fibre 4.3g; Sodium 9mg

Potatoes and parsnips with garlic and cream

For the best results, cut the potatoes and parsnips very thinly – use a mandolin if you have one. This bake takes the strain from a Sunday lunch as it cooks gently in the oven, so serve it with a casserole for a stress-free Sunday morning, or with any roast meat.

Serves 4–6

3 large potatoes, total weight about 675g/1½lb

350g/12oz small to medium-sized parsnips

200ml/7fl oz/scant 1 cup single (light) cream

100ml/3½fl oz/scant ½ cup milk

2 garlic cloves, crushed

butter, for greasing

about 5ml/1 tsp freshly grated nutmeg

75g/3oz/¾ cup coarsely grated Cheddar or Red Leicester cheese

salt and ground black pepper

4 Arrange the potatoes and parsnips in the dish, sprinkling each layer with a little freshly grated nutmeg, salt and ground black pepper

5 Pour the liquid into the dish and press the potatoes and parsnips down into it. Cover with lightly buttered foil and cook in the hot oven for 45 minutes.

6 Remove the foil and sprinkle the grated cheese over the vegetables in an even layer.

7 Return the dish to the oven and continue cooking, uncovered, for a further 20–30 minutes, or until the potatoes and parsnips are tender and the top is golden brown.

1 Peel the potatoes and parsnips and cut them into thin slices. Cook in a large pan of salted boiling water for 5 minutes. Drain and cool slightly.

2 Meanwhile, pour the cream and milk into a heavy pan and add the crushed garlic. Bring to the boil over a medium heat, then remove from the heat and leave to stand for about 10 minutes.

3 Preheat the oven to 180°C/350°F/ Gas 4 and lightly butter the bottom and sides of a shallow ovenproof dish.

Energy 241kcal/1012kJ; Protein 7.8g; Carbohydrate 27.2g, of which sugars 6.4g; Fat 11.7g, of which saturates 7.2g; Cholesterol 31mg; Calcium 173mg; Fibre 3.9g; Sodium 126mg

Mashed potatoes

The potato arrived in England in the latter half of the 16th century and, at first, was treated with great caution. Fluffy mashed potatoes are ideal to eat with casseroles and braises, as they soak up all the delicious sauce.

Serves 4

1kg/2¼lb floury potatoes, such as Maris Piper

about 150ml/¼pint/⅔ cup milk

115g/4oz/½ cup soft butter

salt

freshly grated nutmeg (optional)

1 Peel the potatoes and cook them whole in a large pan of boiling water for about 20 minutes or until soft throughout. Drain. Warm the milk and butter in a large pan.

2 Push the warm potatoes through a ricer, pass them through a mouli, or mash with a potato masher or fork.

3 Add the mashed potato to the milk and beat with a wooden spoon, adding extra milk if necessary to achieve the desired consistency. Season to taste with salt and a little nutmeg (if using).

Variations Cook a small onion, quartered, with the potatoes and mash it with them, or add a spoonful of English (hot) mustard or horseradish sauce to the mash.

Roast potatoes

Roast potatoes can be cooked around a joint of meat, where they will absorb the juices. For crisp potatoes with a soft, fluffy interior, roast them in a separate dish in a single layer.

Serves 4

1.3kg/3lb floury potatoes

90ml/6 tbsp oil, lard or goose fat

salt

1 Preheat the oven to 200°C/400°F/ Gas 6. Peel the potatoes and cut into chunks. Boil in salted water for about 5 minutes, drain, return to the pan, and shake them to roughen the surfaces.

2 Put the fat into a large roasting pan and put into the hot oven to heat the fat. Add the potatoes, coating them in the fat. Return to the oven and cook for 40–50 minutes, turning once or twice, until crisp and cooked through.

Energy 338kcal/1424kJ; Protein 5.9g; Carbohydrate 50.4g, of which sugars 3.3g; Fat 14g, of which saturates 9.1g; Cholesterol 39mg; Calcium 42mg; Fibre 3.6g; Sodium 140mg

Energy 484kcal/2048kJ; Protein 9.4g; Carbohydrate 84.2g, of which sugars 2g; Fat 14.6g, of which saturates 5.9g; Cholesterol 13mg; Calcium 26mg; Fibre 5.9g; Sodium 29mg

Griddle potatoes

This attractive dish has traditionally been cooked with leftover cooked potatoes that have been boiled in their skins. It makes a tasty accompaniment to grilled meat or fish or can be served as a main course with braised cabbage, roast parsnips and cauliflower cheese.

Serves 4–6

2 onions, peeled and chopped

450–675g/1lb–1½lb whole cooked potatoes, boiled in their skins

a mixture of butter and oil, for shallow frying

salt and ground black pepper

1 Put the onions in a large pan and scald them briefly in boiling water. Refresh under cold water and drain well. Peel and slice the potatoes.

2 Put a mixture of butter and oil into a large, heavy frying pan and heat well.

3 When the fat is hot, fry the onion until tender. Add the potato slices and brown them together, turning the potato slices to brown as evenly as possible on both sides. Transfer to a warmed serving dish and season with salt and pepper. Serve very hot.

Energy 163Kcal/681kJ; Protein 3.4g; Carbohydrate 26.4g, of which sugars 5g; Fat 5.5g, of which saturates 3.3g; Cholesterol 13mg; Calcium 26mg; Fibre 2.6g; Sodium 49mg

Puddings and Desserts

Everyone loves a pudding, and the English have many variations to enjoy, even if it's only as an occasional treat. Orchard fruits are often a main ingredient – stewed or baked and made into tarts, crumbles and pies. There are also nursery-style puds made with sponge, suet pastry, bread, rice or batter, as well as rich, creamy concoctions made with products from the dairy.

Treacle tart

The name of this tart is somewhat misleading, since golden syrup, not treacle or molasses, is used for the filling. This is one of those puddings that people can always find space for even after a generous main course. Serve it warm or cold, with custard or cream.

3 Mix the breadcrumbs with the ginger, if using, and spread the mixture over the bottom of the pastry. Gently warm the syrup with the lemon rind and juice (on the stove or in the microwave) until quite runny and pour evenly over the breadcrumbs.

4 Gather the reserved pastry trimmings into a ball, roll out on a lightly floured surface and cut into long, narrow strips. Twist these into spirals and arrange them in a lattice pattern on top of the tart, pressing them on to the edge to secure. Trim the ends.

5 Put into the hot oven and cook for about 25 minutes until the pastry is golden brown and cooked through and the filling has set.

Variation Omit the lemon rind and juice if you prefer. Sometimes finely crushed cornflakes are used in place of the breadcrumbs.

Serves 6

175g/6oz/1½ cups plain (all-purpose) flour

pinch of salt

40g/1½oz/3 tbsp lard

40g/1½oz/3 tbsp butter, diced

75g/3oz/1½ cups fresh breadcrumbs

2.5ml/½ tsp ground ginger (optional)

225g/8oz/1 cup golden (corn) syrup

grated rind and juice of 1 lemon

1 Sift the flour and salt into a bowl and add the lard and butter. With the fingertips, rub the fats into the flour until the mixture resembles fine breadcrumbs. Stir in about 45ml/3 tbsp cold water until the mixture can be gathered together into a smooth ball of dough. Wrap the pastry and refrigerate for 30 minutes. Meanwhile, preheat the oven to 190°C/375°F/Gas 5.

2 Roll out the pastry on a lightly floured surface and use to line a 20cm/8in flan tin (pan) or pie plate, reserving the trimmings.

Energy 420kcal/1764kJ; Protein 4.1g; Carbohydrate 63.5g, of which sugars 35.1g; Fat 18.4g, of which saturates 11.3g; Cholesterol 46mg; Calcium 62mg; Fibre 1.1g; Sodium 344mg

Bakewell tart

This is a modern version of the Bakewell pudding, said to be the result of a 19th-century kitchen accident and still baked in the original shop in Bakewell, Derbyshire. This very popular, tart-like version is simpler to make and is a favourite Sunday lunch dessert.

Serves 4

For the pastry

115g/4oz/1 cup plain (all-purpose) flour

pinch of salt

50g/2oz/4 tbsp butter, diced

For the filling

30ml/2 tbsp raspberry or apricot jam

2 whole eggs and 2 extra yolks

115g/4oz/generous ½ cup caster (superfine) sugar

115g/4oz/½ cup butter, melted

55g/2oz/⅔ cup ground almonds

few drops of almond extract

icing (confectioners') sugar, to dust

1 Sift the flour and salt and rub in the butter until the mixture resembles fine crumbs. Stir in about 20ml/2 tbsp cold water and gather into a smooth ball of dough. Wrap and chill for 30 minutes. Preheat the oven to 200°C/400°F/Gas 6.

2 Roll out the pastry and use to line an 18cm/7in loose-based flan tin (pan). Spread the jam over the pastry.

3 Whisk the eggs, egg yolks and sugar together in a large bowl until the mixture is thick and pale.

4 Gently stir in the melted butter, ground almonds and almond extract.

5 Pour the mixture over the jam in the pastry case (pie shell). Put the tart into the hot oven and cook for 30 minutes until just set and browned. Sift a little icing sugar over the top before serving warm or at room temperature.

Energy 700kcal/2919kJ; Protein 10.8g; Carbohydrate 57.1g, of which sugars 36.7g; Fat 49.9g, of which saturates 17.1g; Cholesterol 257mg; Calcium 110mg; Fibre 0.9g; Sodium 394mg

Lemon meringue pie

This popular dessert is a 20th-century development of older English cheesecakes – open tarts with a filling of curds. It was particularly relished in the 1950s after the years of wartime rationing, when sugar, lemons and eggs became plentiful. It is best served at room temperature, so makes a good Sunday lunch dessert as it can be baked in advance.

Serves 6

For the pastry

115g/4oz/1 cup plain (all-purpose) flour

pinch of salt

25g/1oz/2 tbsp lard, diced

25g/1oz/2 tbsp butter, diced

For the filling

50g/2oz/¼ cup cornflour (cornstarch)

175g/6oz/¾ cup caster (superfine) sugar

finely grated rind and juice of 2 lemons

2 egg yolks

15g/½oz/1 tbsp butter, diced

For the meringue topping

2 egg whites

75g/3oz/½ cup caster (superfine) sugar

1 To make the pastry, sift the flour and salt into a bowl and add the lard and butter. With the fingertips, lightly rub the fats into the flour until the mixture resembles fine crumbs.

2 Stir in about 20ml/2 tbsp cold water until the mixture can be gathered together into a smooth ball of dough. (Alternatively make the pastry using a food processor.) Wrap the pastry and refrigerate for at least 30 minutes. Meanwhile, preheat the oven to 200°C/400°F/Gas 6.

3 Roll out the pastry on a lightly floured surface and use to line a 20cm/8in flan tin (pan). Prick the base with a fork, line with baking parchment or foil and add a layer of baking beans to prevent the pastry rising.

4 Put the pastry case (pie shell) into the hot oven and cook for 15 minutes. Remove the beans and parchment or foil, return the pastry to the oven and cook for a further 5 minutes until crisp and golden brown. Reduce the oven temperature to 150°C/300°F/Gas 2.

5 To make the lemon filling, put the cornflour into a pan and add the sugar, lemon rind and 300ml/½ pint/ 1¼ cups water. Heat the mixture, stirring continuously, until it comes to the boil and thickens. Reduce the heat and simmer very gently for 1 minute. Remove the pan from the heat and stir in the lemon juice.

6 Add the the egg yolks to the lemon mixture, one at a time and beating after each addition, and then stir in the butter. Tip the mixture into the baked pastry case and level the surface.

7 To make the meringue topping, whisk the egg whites until stiff peaks form then whisk in half the sugar. Fold in the rest of the sugar using a metal spoon.

8 Spread the meringue over the lemon filling, covering it completely. Cook for about 20 minutes until lightly browned.

Energy 357kcal/1497kJ; Protein 6.8g; Carbohydrate 42.8g, of which sugars 25.1g; Fat 18.9g, of which saturates 9g; Cholesterol 129mg; Calcium 108mg; Fibre 0.7g; Sodium 137mg

Syrup sponge pudding

England is famous for its steamed puddings and this one is a classic. The light sponge with its golden coat of syrup brings back memories of childhood when, for many, syrup sponge pudding (probably in a more stodgy version) was a of the highlights of school dinners. Serve this one with freshly made custard or cold pouring cream.

Serves 4–6

45ml/3 tbsp golden (light corn) syrup

115g/4oz/8 tbsp soft butter

115g/4oz/½ cup caster (superfine) sugar

2 eggs

5ml/1 tsp finely grated lemon rind

175g/6oz/1½ cups self-raising (self-rising) flour

30ml/2 tbsp milk

1 Butter a 1.2 litre/2 pint/5 cup heatproof bowl and spoon the golden syrup into the bottom of it.

2 In a large bowl, beat the butter and sugar until pale, light and fluffy.

3 In a separate bowl, beat the eggs and then gradually beat them into the butter-and-sugar mixture together with the lemon rind.

Variations Replace the golden syrup with orange or lemon marmalade, or jam such as raspberry or plum.
• Add a few drops of vanilla extract to the sponge mixture in place of the lemon rind.

4 Sift the flour over the mixture and fold it in lightly using a metal spoon. Gently stir in the milk to give a soft dropping consistency.

5 Spoon the sponge mixture over the golden syrup in the bowl.

6 Cover the pudding with a sheet of greaseproof (waxed) paper or baking parchment, making a pleat in the centre to give the pudding room to rise. Cover this with a large sheet of foil (again pleated in the centre).

7 Tie a length of string securely around the bowl, under the lip, to hold the foil and paper in place.

8 Half-fill a large pan with water and bring it to the boil. Place an inverted saucer or trivet in the bottom and stand the bowl on it. Cover the pan and steam the pudding for about 1½ hours, topping up the pan with more boiling water if necessary.

9 Remove the pudding from the steamer and leave it standing for about 5 minutes before turning out on to a warm plate to serve.

Cook's tips To cook the pudding in the microwave, cover the bowl with baking parchment (but do not tie it on) and cook on medium (500–600W) for 6–8 minutes until the sponge is just cooked through. Leave to stand for 5 minutes before serving.
• The pudding can also be baked for a drier, cakier texture. Preheat the oven to 190°C/375°F/Gas 5. Cover the bowl with buttered foil and cook for 35–40 minutes. Meanwhile, heat 45ml/3tbsp golden syrup gently with 30ml/2tbsp water. Pour this hot sauce into a jug (pitcher) and serve alongside the pudding for pouring over.

Energy 480kcal/2005kJ; Protein 16.2g; Carbohydrate 48.2g, of which sugars 23.7g; Fat 27g, of which saturates 15.8g; Cholesterol 173mg; Calcium 153mg; Fibre 1.2g; Sodium 451mg

Christmas pudding

Plum pudding and figgy pudding were the forerunners of today's concoction of mixed dried fruits. This pudding is eaten on Christmas Day, brought to the table doused in warm brandy or whisky and set alight. Serve with pouring cream and brandy butter.

Makes 2 puddings, each serving 6–8

280g/10oz/5 cups fresh breadcrumbs

225g/8oz/1 cup light muscovado (brown) sugar

225g/8oz/1 cup currants

280g/10oz/2 cups raisins

225g/8oz/1⅓ cups sultanas (golden raisins)

50g/2oz/⅓ cup chopped (candied) mixed peel

115g/4oz/½ cup glacé (candied) cherries

225g/8oz suet, shredded (or vegetarian equivalent)

2.5ml/½ tsp salt

10–20ml/2–4 tsp mixed (apple pie) spice

1 carrot, peeled and coarsely grated

1 apple, peeled, cored and finely chopped

grated rind and juice of 1 orange

2 large eggs, lightly whisked

450ml/¾ pint/scant 2 cups stout

butter, for greasing

1 Put the breadcrumbs, sugar, dried fruit and peel in a large mixing bowl. Add the suet, salt, mixed spice, carrot, apple and orange rind. Mix well.

Cook's tip When a pudding is required, steam it for another 2-3 hours and serve hot. Christmas puddings are made at least a month in advance (traditionally on "stir-up Sunday" at the end of November).

2 Stir the orange juice, eggs and stout into the breadcrumbs. Leave overnight, stirring occasionally, if possible.

3 Butter two 1.2 litre/2 pint/5 cup heatproof bowls and put a circle of baking parchment in the bottoms. Stir the mixture and turn into the bowls.

4 Top with buttered circles of baking parchment, cover tightly with more layers of parchment and foil, tied securely under the rim. Steam for about 6–7 hours, top with boiling water as necessary. When the puddings are cooked and cooled, re-cover them with foil and store in a cool, dry place.

Energy 448kcal/1902kJ; Protein 2.4g; Carbohydrate 99.8g, of which sugars 92.5g; Fat 7.1g, of which saturates 3.6g; Cholesterol 20mg; Calcium 67mg; Fibre 0.9g; Sodium 123mg

Baked rice pudding

Rice pudding can be traced back to medieval England, when rice and sugar were expensive imports. Much later it was recommended for nursing mothers and became a nursery favourite, served with jam. This is a filling dessert best served after a lighter main course.

Serves 4

50g/2oz/4 tbsp butter, diced, plus extra for greasing

50g/2oz/¼ cup pudding rice

30ml/2 tbsp soft light brown sugar

900ml/1½ pints/3¾ cups milk

small strip of lemon rind

freshly grated nutmeg

Variations Add some sultanas (golden raisins), raisins or ready-to-eat dried apricots and cinnamon to the pudding.
• Serve with fresh fruit such as sliced peaches, raspberries or strawberries.

1 Preheat the oven to 150°C/300°F/ Gas 2. Butter a 1.2 litre/2 pint/5 cup shallow ovenproof dish.

2 Put the rice, sugar and butter into the dish and stir in the milk. Add the strip of lemon rind and sprinkle a little nutmeg over the surface. Put the pudding into the hot oven.

3 Cook the pudding for about 2 hours, stirring after 30 minutes and another couple of times during the next 1½ hours, until the rice is tender and the pudding is thick and creamy.

4 If you prefer skin on top, leave the pudding undisturbed for the final 30 minutes, or stir again. Serve with jam.

Energy 298kcal/1252kJ; Protein 8.8g; Carbohydrate 54.3g, of which sugars 21.5g; Fat 5.2g, of which saturates 1.4g; Cholesterol 143mg; Calcium 71mg; Fibre 0g; Sodium 185mg

Jam roly poly

This warming winter pudding, with its nursery-sounding name, first appeared on English tables in the 1800s. While boiling is the traditional cooking method for jam roly poly, baking produces a lovely crisp golden crust and a sticky jam filling. This is another seriously filling pudding, that should be served in small portions or after a light main course.

Serves 4–6

175g/6oz/1½ cups self-raising (self-rising) flour

pinch of salt

75g/3oz shredded suet (or vegetarian equivalent)

finely grated rind of 1 small lemon

90ml/6 tbsp jam

1 Preheat the oven to 180°C/350°F/Gas 4 and line a baking sheet with baking parchment.

2 Sift the flour and salt into a bowl and stir in the suet and lemon rind. With a round-ended knife, stir in just enough cold water to enable you to gather the mixture into a ball of soft dough, finishing off with your fingers.

3 Remove the ball of dough from the bowl, and on a lightly floured work surface or board, knead it very lightly until smooth.

Cook's tip For the lightest suet pastry, use as little cold water as possible to mix the dough, and handle it as gently and lightly as you can.

4 Gently roll out the pastry into a rectangle that measures approximately 30 x 20cm/12 x 8in.

5 Using a palette knife or metal spatula, spread the jam evenly over the pastry, leaving the side edges and ends clear.

6 Brush the edges of the pastry with a little water and, starting at one of the short ends, carefully roll up the pastry. Try to keep the roll fairly loose so that the jam is not squeezed out.

7 Place the roll, seam side down, on the prepared baking sheet. Put into the hot oven and cook for 30–40 minutes until risen, golden brown and cooked through. Leave the pudding to cool for a few minutes before cutting into thick slices to serve.

Variation To make a similar traditional nursery favourite, Spotted Dick, replace half the flour with 115g/4oz/2 cups fresh white breadcrumbs; add 50g/2oz/¼ cup caster (superfine) sugar and 175g/6oz/¾ cup currants to the flour in step 2. Instead of water to mix, use about 75ml/5 tbsp milk. Leave out the jam and just form into a sausage shape without rolling.

To boil the roly poly
1 Shape the mixture into a roll and wrap loosely (to allow room for the pudding to rise) first in baking parchment and then in a large sheet of foil. Twist the ends of the paper and foil to seal them securely and tie a string handle from one end to the other.

2 Lower the package into a wide pan of boiling water on the stove, cover and boil for about 1½ hours. Check the water level occasionally and top up with boiling water if necessary.

Energy 240kcal/1008kJ; Protein 2.8g; Carbohydrate 33.7g, of which sugars 10.7g; Fat 11.3g, of which saturates 5.7g; Cholesterol 0mg; Calcium 104mg; Fibre 0.9g; Sodium 111mg

Eve's pudding

The name "Mother Eve's pudding", from the biblical Eve, was first used in the 19th century for a boiled suet pudding filled with apples, from which this lighter sponge version developed.

Serves 4–6

115g/4oz/½ cup butter

115g/4oz/½ cup caster (superfine) sugar

2 eggs, beaten

grated rind and juice of 1 lemon

90g/3¼oz/scant 1 cup self-raising (self-rising) flour

40g/1½oz/⅓ cup ground almonds

115g/4oz/scant ½ cup brown sugar

550–675g/1¼–1½lb cooking apples, cored and thinly sliced

25g/1oz/¼ cup flaked (sliced) almonds

1 Preheat the oven to 180°C/350°F/ Gas 4. Beat together the butter and caster sugar in a large mixing bowl until the mixture is very light and fluffy.

2 Gradually beat the eggs into the butter mixture, beating well after each addition, then fold in the lemon rind, flour and ground almonds.

3 Mix the brown sugar, apples and lemon juice and tip the mixture into an ovenproof dish, spreading it out evenly.

4 Spoon the sponge mixture over the top in an even layer and right to the edges. Sprinkle the almonds over. Put into the hot oven and cook for 40–45 minutes until risen and golden brown.

Energy 507kcal/2128kJ; Protein 6.9g; Carbohydrate 65.5g, of which sugars 52.7g; Fat 26.1g, of which saturates 12g; Cholesterol 114mg; Calcium 91mg; Fibre 2.8g; Sodium 159mg

Yorkshire lemon surprise

During cooking a tangy lemon sauce collects beneath a light sponge topping. It's important to bake this dish when it is standing in the bath of hot water, otherwise it will not work.

Serves 4

50g/2oz/¼ cup butter, plus extra for greasing

grated rind and juice of 2 lemons

115g/4oz/½ cup caster (superfine) sugar

2 eggs, separated

50g/2oz/½ cup self-raising (self-rising) flour

300ml/½ pint/1¼ cups milk

1 Preheat the oven to 190°C/375°F/ Gas 5. Use a little butter to grease a 1.2 litre/2 pint/5 cup ovenproof dish.

2 Beat the remaining butter, lemon rind and caster sugar in a bowl until pale and fluffy. Add the egg yolks and flour and beat together well. Gradually whisk in the lemon juice and milk (the mixture may curdle horribly, but don't be alarmed). In a clean bowl, whisk the egg whites until they form stiff peaks.

3 Fold the egg whites lightly into the lemon mixture using a metal spoon, then pour into the prepared dish.

4 Place the dish in a roasting pan pour in hot water to fill halfway up the sides, put into the hot oven and cook for 45 minutes until golden.

Energy 319kcal/1341kJ; Protein 7g; Carbohydrate 43.1g, of which sugars 33.8g; Fat 14.5g, of which saturates 8.1g; Cholesterol 126mg; Calcium 166mg; Fibre 0.4g; Sodium 190mg

Apple and blackberry crumble

The origins of crumble are unclear. It did not appear in recipe books until the 20th century, but has become a favourite Sunday lunch dessert all over the country. Autumn heralds the apple harvest and their perfect partners, blackberries. The oatmeal adds delicious crunch.

Serves 6–8

115g/4oz/½ cup butter

115g/4oz/1 cup wholemeal (whole-wheat) flour

50g/2oz/½ cup fine or medium oatmeal

50g/2oz/¼ cup soft light brown sugar

a little grated lemon rind (optional)

900g/2lb cooking apples

450g/1lb/4 cups blackberries

squeeze of lemon juice

175g/6oz/scant 1 cup caster (superfine) sugar

1 Preheat the oven to 200°C/400°F/Gas 6. To make the crumble, rub the butter into the flour, and then add the oatmeal and brown sugar and continue to rub in until the mixture begins to stick together, forming large crumbs.

2 Mix in the grated lemon rind if using. Peel and core the cooking apples and slice into wedges.

3 Put the apples, blackberries, lemon juice, 30ml/2 tbsp water and caster sugar in a shallow ovenproof dish, about 2 litres/3½ pints/9 cups capacity.

4 Cover the fruit with the crumble topping. Put into the hot oven and cook for 15 minutes, then reduce the heat to 190°C/375°F/Gas 5 and cook for 15–20 minutes until golden brown.

Energy 336kcal/1413kJ; Protein 4g; Carbohydrate 53.1g, of which sugars 30.8g; Fat 13.4g, of which saturates 6.8g; Cholesterol 27mg; Calcium 72mg; Fibre 3g; Sodium 81mg

Winter fruit crumble

This crumble uses pears and dried fruit in its base, making it ideal for the winter months. Serve it with custard or whipped cream. At other times of the year, try gooseberries or rhubarb flavoured with orange zest. The almond topping adds a delicious rich texture.

Serves 6

175g/6oz/1½ cups plain (all-purpose) flour

50g/2oz/½ cup ground almonds

175g/6oz/¾ cup butter, diced

115g/4oz/½ cup soft light brown sugar

40g/1½oz flaked (sliced) almonds

1 orange

about 16 ready-to-eat dried apricots

4 firm ripe pears

1 Preheat the oven to 190°C/375°F/ Gas 5. To make the topping, sift the flour into a bowl and stir in the ground almonds. Add the butter and rub it into the flour until the mixture resembles rough breadcrumbs. Stir in 75g/3oz/ ⅓ cup sugar and the flaked almonds.

2 Finely grate 5ml/1 tsp rind from the orange and squeeze out its juice. Halve the apricots and put them into a shallow ovenproof dish. Peel the pears, remove their cores and cut the fruit into small pieces. Scatter the pears over the apricots. Stir the orange rind into the orange juice and sprinkle over the fruit. Scatter the remaining brown sugar over the top.

3 Cover the fruit completely with the crumble mixture and smooth over. Put into the hot oven and cook for about 40 minutes until the topping is golden brown and the fruit is soft (test with the point of a sharp knife).

Energy 615kcal/2569kJ; Protein 9.4g; Carbohydrate 65.7g, of which sugars 42.9g; Fat 36.7g, of which saturates 16.2g; Cholesterol 62mg; Calcium 150mg; Fibre 6.6g; Sodium 190mg

Bread and butter pudding

Plates of white bread and butter were for many years a standard feature of an English lunch or supper, when frugal cooks needed to come up with ways to use up the leftovers. Bread and butter pudding was a family favourite until, surprisingly, in the late 20th century it was given a makeover using cream and brioche and began to appear on the menus of upmarket restaurants. This is the original version, which traditionalists prefer.

Serves 4–6

50g/2oz/4 tbsp soft butter

about 6 large slices of day-old white bread

50g/2oz dried fruit, such as raisins, sultanas (golden raisins) or chopped dried apricots

40g/1½oz/3 tbsp caster (superfine) sugar

2 large eggs

600ml/1 pint/2½ cups full cream (whole) milk

1 Preheat the oven to 160°C/325°F/ Gas 5. Lightly butter a 1.2 litre/2 pint/5 cup ovenproof dish.

2 Butter the slices of bread and cut them into small triangles or squares.

3 Arrange half the bread pieces, buttered side up, in the prepared dish and sprinkle the dried fruit and half of the sugar over the top.

4 Lay the remaining bread slices, again buttered side up, evenly on top of the fruit. Sprinkle the remaining sugar evenly over the top.

5 Beat the eggs lightly together, just to break up the yolks and whites, and stir in the milk.

6 Strain the egg mixture and pour it over the bread in the dish. Push the top slices down into the liquid if necessary so that it is evenly absorbed.

7 Leave the pudding to stand for 30 minutes to allow the bread to soak up all the liquid (this is an important step so don't be tempted to skip it).

8 Put the dish into the hot oven and cook for about 45 minutes or until the custard is set and the top is crisp and golden brown. Serve the pudding immediately with pouring cream.

Variation To make a special occasion chocolate bread and butter pudding, complete steps 1–4, omitting the dried fruit if you wish. Break 150g/5oz dark (bittersweet) chocolate into 500ml/ 17fl oz/generous 2 cups milk and heat gently (on the stove or on low power in the microwave) until the milk is warm and the chocolate has melted. Stir frequently during heating and do not allow the milk to boil. Stir the warm chocolate milk into the beaten eggs in step 5, and then continue with the remaining steps.
• You could replace the dried fruit in either version of the pudding with slices of fresh banana.

Energy 622kcal/2597kJ; Protein 10.5g; Carbohydrate 55.6g, of which sugars 37.8g; Fat 39g, of which saturates 23g; Cholesterol 186mg; Calcium 203mg; Fibre 1.6g; Sodium 350mg

Baked apples with mincemeat

This quintessential British fruit was once thought to have magical powers and, to this day, apples are linked with many English traditions and festivals. Here, they are baked in the oven with a filling of sweetened dried fruit, and make a perfect end to a rich Sunday lunch. They are best served straight from the oven, before they begin to crumple.

Serves 4

25g/1oz/2 tbsp butter, plus extra for greasing

4 cooking apples

about 60ml/4 tbsp mincemeat

30ml/2 tbsp honey

1 Preheat the oven to 180°C/350°F/ Gas 4. Butter a shallow ovenproof dish.

Variation Replace the mincemeat with chopped dried apricots or dates.

2 With an apple corer or a small sharp knife, remove the cores from the apples. Run a sharp knife around the middle of each apple, cutting through the skin but not deep into the flesh. Stand the apples in the dish.

3 Fill the hollow centres of the apples with mincemeat. Drizzle the honey over the top and dot with butter. Add 60ml/4 tbsp water to the dish. Bake for about 45 minutes until soft throughout, and serve at once.

Energy 70kcal/301kJ; Protein 0.7g; Carbohydrate 17.4g, of which sugars 17.4g; Fat 0.3g, of which saturates 0g; Cholesterol 0mg; Calcium 30mg; Fibre 2.4g; Sodium 9mg

Poached spiced pears

These succulent spiced pears make a light and elegant end to a Sunday lunch, they are also easy for the cook to make in advance, and left to stand while the main course is eaten. The pears can be served warm or at room temperature, and are delicious served with cream and perhaps some crisp, sweet biscuits for a contrast in texture.

Serves 4

115g/4oz/½ cup caster (superfine) sugar

grated rind and juice of 1 lemon

2.5ml/½ tsp ground ginger

1 small cinnamon stick

2 whole cloves

4 firm ripe pears

Variations Omit the spices and instead flavour the water with ginger or elderflower cordial.
• Use white wine in place of water.

1 Put the sugar in a pan with 300ml/ ½ pint/1½ cups water, the lemon rind and juice, ginger and spices. Heat, stirring, until the sugar has dissolved.

2 Peel the pears, cut them in half lengthways and remove their cores.

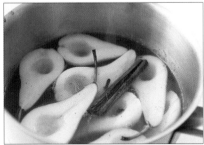

3 Add the pear halves to the pan and bring just to the boil. Cover and simmer gently for about 5 minutes or until the pears are tender, turning them over in the syrup occasionally during cooking. Remove from the heat and leave to cool in the syrup before serving.

Energy 93kcal/392kJ; Protein 0.5g; Carbohydrate 23.6g, of which sugars 23.6g; Fat 0.2g, of which saturates 0g; Cholesterol 0mg; Calcium 17mg; Fibre 3.3g; Sodium 6mg

Eton mess

The "mess" consists of whipped cream, crushed meringue and sliced or mashed strawberries, and is an easy summer-time dessert. The pudding gets its name from the famous public school, Eton College, where it is served at the annual picnic on 4 June.

Serves 4

450g/1lb ripe strawberries

45ml/3 tbsp elderflower cordial or orange liqueur

300ml/½ pint/1¼ cups double (heavy) cream

4 meringues or meringue baskets

Cook's tips Serve Eton mess just as it is or accompanied by crisp sweet biscuits (cookies).
• Make the dish with other soft fruit, such as lightly crushed raspberries or blackcurrants.
• This is a useful recipe to know if you are trying to make a large meringue and it cracks, as you can just break it up completely and serve it this way.

1 Remove the green hulls from the strawberries and slice the fruit into a bowl, reserving a few for decoration.

2 Sprinkle with the elderflower cordial or fruit liqueur. Cover the bowl and chill for about 2 hours.

3 Whip the cream until soft peaks form. Crush the meringue into small pieces. Add the fruit and most of the meringue to the cream and fold in lightly. Spoon into serving dishes and chill until required. Before serving, decorate with the reserved strawberries and meringue.

Energy 526kcal/2182kJ; Protein 3.5g; Carbohydrate 32.8g, of which sugars 32.8g; Fat 40.4g, of which saturates 25.1g; Cholesterol 103mg; Calcium 60mg; Fibre 1.4g; Sodium 53mg

Devonshire junket

Junkets, or curds, were eaten by the medieval nobility and became universally popular in Tudor England. Junket is also known as damask cream, perhaps because of its silky consistency. This makes a sophisticated end to a quintessentially English Sunday lunch.

Serves 4

600ml/1 pint/2½ cups milk

45ml/3 tbsp caster (superfine) sugar

several drops of triple-strength rosewater

10ml/2 tsp rennet

60ml/4 tbsp double (heavy) cream

sugared rose petals, to decorate (optional)

1 Gently heat the milk with 30ml/2 tbsp of the sugar, stirring, until the sugar has dissolved and the temperature reaches body heat (37°C/98.4°F).

2 Remove from the heat and stir in rosewater to taste, then the rennet.

Cook's tip You must use fresh milk for junket, it will not set properly if homogenized or UHT milk is used. Whole milk also gives a better flavour.

3 Pour the junket into serving dishes and leave undisturbed at room temperature for 2–3 hours, until set. Do not move it during this time, otherwise it will separate into curds and whey.

4 Stir the remaining sugar into the cream, then carefully spoon the mixture over the surface of the set junket. Decorate with sugared rose petals, if you wish.

Energy 196kcal/824kJ; Protein 7.5g; Carbohydrate 19.1g, of which sugars 19.1g; Fat 10.6g, of which saturates 6.6g; Cholesterol 29mg; Calcium 193mg; Fibre 0g; Sodium 69mg

Summer pudding

This stunning dessert is an essential part of the English summer and it is deceptively simple to make. Use a mixture of fresh seasonal soft fruits and a good quality loaf of white bread. Serve the pudding cold with lashings of thick cream or yogurt.

2 Place all the fruit in a pan with the sugar. Do not add any water. Cook very gently for 4–5 minutes until the juices begin to run.

3 Allow the mixture to cool then spoon the berries, and enough of their juices to moisten the fruit, into the bread-lined bowl. Reserve any remaining juice to serve with the pudding.

4 Fold over the excess bread, then cover the fruit with the remaining slices, trimming to fit. Place a small plate or saucer that fits inside the bowl directly on top of the pudding. Weight it down with a 900g/2lb weight, if you have one, or use a couple of full food cans.

5 Chill the pudding in the refrigerator for at least 8 hours or overnight. To serve, run a knife between the pudding and the bowl and turn out onto a plate. Spoon any reserved juices over the top, and serve with cream or yogurt.

Serves 4–6

about 8 x 1cm/½in-thick slices of day-old white bread, with crusts removed

800g/1¾lb/6–7 cups mixed berries, such as strawberries, raspberries, blackcurrants, redcurrants and blueberries

50g/2oz/¼ cup golden caster (superfine) sugar

lightly whipped double (heavy) cream or thick yogurt, to serve

1 Trim a slice of bread to fit neatly in the base of a 1.2 litre/2 pint/5 cup bowl, then trim another 5–6 slices to line the sides, making sure the bread stands up above the rim.

Energy 192kcal/815kJ; Protein 5.2g; Carbohydrate 43.1g, of which sugars 22.1g; Fat 1g, of which saturates 0g; Cholesterol 0mg; Calcium 82mg; Fibre 2.5g; Sodium 245mg

Gooseberry and elderflower fool

Little can be simpler than swirling cooked fresh fruit into whipped cream. Rhubarb is another favourite seasonal flavour to use in this recipe. Be sure to serve fool in pretty glasses or dishes, accompanied by crisp biscuits to add a contrast of texture.

Serves 4

500g/1¼lb gooseberries

300ml/½ pint/1¼ cups double (heavy) cream

about 115g/4oz/1 cup icing (confectioners') sugar, to taste

30ml/2 tbsp elderflower cordial

mint sprigs, to decorate

crisp biscuits (cookies), to serve

1 Place the gooseberries in a heavy saucepan, cover and cook over a low heat, shaking the pan occasionally, until tender. Tip the gooseberries into a bowl, crush them with a fork or potato masher, then leave to cool completely.

2 Whip the cream until soft peaks form, then fold in half the crushed fruit. Add sugar and elderflower cordial to taste. Sweeten the remaining fruit to taste.

3 Layer the cream mixture and the crushed gooseberries in four dessert dishes or tall glasses, then cover and chill until ready to serve. Decorate the fool with mint sprigs and serve with crisp sweet biscuits.

Variations When elderflowers are in season, cook 2–3 elderflower heads with the gooseberries and omit the elderflower cordial.
• For rhubarb fool use squeezed orange juice in place of elderflower cordial.

Energy 366kcal/1521kJ; Protein 3.5g; Carbohydrate 24.2g, of which sugars 21.8g; Fat 28.4g, of which saturates 16.7g; Cholesterol 70mg; Calcium 111mg; Fibre 1.9g; Sodium 41mg

Fruit and wine jelly

In 17th-century England, when making jelly was a lengthy process it was a centrepiece at high-class banquets. Though jelly now tends to be associated with children's parties it can still make a light and elegant dessert for a summer Sunday lunch. You need to allow plenty of time for sieving the fruit and cooling the jelly, so it's ideal for making in advance.

Serves 6

600g/1lb 6oz fresh raspberries

140g/5oz/¾ cup white sugar

300ml/½ pint/1¼ cups medium-dry white wine

5 sheets of gelatine (6 if the jelly is to be set in a mould and turned out)

Cook's tip Instead of making your own fruit juice, use a carton of juice, such as mango, cranberry or orange, sweetened to taste.

1 Put the raspberries and sugar in a pan with 100ml/3½fl oz/scant ½ cup water and heat gently until the fruit releases its juices and becomes very soft, and the sugar has dissolved.

2 Remove the pan from the heat, tip the mixture into a fine nylon sieve (strainer) or jelly bag over a large bowl, and leave to strain – this will take some time but do not squeeze the fruit or the resulting juice may be cloudy.

3 When the juice from the fruit has drained into the bowl, make it up to 600ml/1 pint/2½ cups with water if necessary. Soak the gelatine in cold water for about 5 minutes to soften it.

4 Heat half the juice until very hot but not quite boiling. Remove from the heat. Squeeze the softened gelatine to remove excess water, then stir it into the hot juice until dissolved. Stir in the remaining raspberry juice and the wine.

5 Pour into stemmed glasses and chill until set. Alternatively, set the jelly in a wetted mould and turn out onto a pretty plate for serving.

Energy 178kcal/758kJ; Protein 8.6g; Carbohydrate 29.3g, of which sugars 29.3g; Fat 0.3g, of which saturates 0.1g; Cholesterol 0mg; Calcium 42mg; Fibre 2.5g; Sodium 6mg.

Almond and rosewater blancmange

In the Middle Ages blancmange (literally "white food") was a banqueting dish that contained chicken and rice as well as almonds and sugar. Later, arrowroot and cornflour were used as thickeners (and indeed are often still used). During Victoria's reign the dessert began to be set with gelatine in fancy moulds and became very fashionable.

Serves 6

5 sheets of gelatine

1 lemon

450ml/¾ pint/1⅔ cups milk

115g/4oz/½ cup caster (superfine) sugar

450ml/¾ pint/scant 2 cups single (light) cream

85g/3oz/¾ cup ground almonds

about 2.5ml/1 tsp triple-strength rosewater

fresh or sugared rose petals, to decorate (optional)

1 Soak the gelatine leaves in cold water for about 5 minutes to soften them.

2 Thinly pare strips of rind from the lemon, taking care not to include the white pith. Heat the milk gently with the lemon rind until it just comes to the boil. Discard the rind.

Variations Omit the lemon rind and add 2.5ml/1 tsp vanilla extract at step 3.
• Instead of rosewater, use your favourite liqueur.

3 Lift the softened sheets of gelatine out of the soaking water, squeezing out the excess. Stir the gelatine into the hot milk until dissolved. Stir in the sugar until it has dissolved. Add the cream, almonds and rosewater to taste and mix well.

4 Pour into one large or six individual wetted moulds, put into the refrigerator and chill until completely set.

5 Turn the blancmange out of its mould(s) just before serving. Decorate with rose petals if you wish.

Energy 350kcal/1462kJ; Protein 10.2g; Carbohydrate 26.2g, of which sugars 25.8g; Fat 23.5g, of which saturates 10.6g; Cholesterol 46mg; Calcium 201mg; Fibre 1.1g; Sodium 57mg

Fruit trifle

Everyone's favourite, trifle is a classic English dessert. The earliest trifles were creamy confections rather like fools, but in the 18th century the dish took the form familiar today, with layers of sponge soaked in wine or sherry, topped with syllabub or whipped cream.

Serves 6–8

1 x 15–18cm/6–7in plain sponge cake

225g/8oz/¾ cup raspberry jam

150ml/¼ pint/⅔ cup medium or sweet sherry

450g/1lb ripe fruit, such as pears and bananas, peeled and sliced

300ml/½ pint/1¼ cups whipping cream

toasted flaked (sliced) almonds, to decorate or glacé (candied) cherries and angelica, (optional)

For the custard

450ml/¾ pint/scant 2 cups full cream (whole) milk

1 vanilla pod (bean)

3 eggs

25g/1oz/2 tbsp caster (superfine) sugar

1 To make the custard, put the milk into a pan with the vanilla pod, split along its length, and bring almost to the boil. Remove from the heat. Leave to cool a little while you whisk the eggs and sugar together lightly. Remove the vanilla pod from the milk and gradually whisk the milk into the egg mixture.

2 Rinse out the pan with cold water and return the mixture to it. (Alternatively, use a double boiler, or a bowl over a pan of boiling water.)

3 Stir over a low heat until it thickens enough to coat the back of a wooden spoon; do not allow the custard to boil. Turn the custard into a bowl, cover and set aside while you assemble the trifle.

4 Halve the sponge cake horizontally, spread with the raspberry jam and sandwich together. Cut into slices and use to line the bottom and lower sides of a large glass serving bowl.

Variation The sherry could be replaced with fruit juice, whisky or a fruit liqueur.

5 Sprinkle the sponge cake with the sherry. Spread the fruit over the sponge in an even layer. Pour the custard on top, cover with clear film (plastic wrap) to prevent a skin forming, and leave to cool and set. Chill until required.

6 To serve, whip the cream and spread it over the custard. Decorate with the almonds, cherries and angelica, if using.

Energy 631kcal/2615kJ; Protein 8.4g; Carbohydrate 24.9g, of which sugars 18.4g; Fat 53.1g, of which saturates 28.4g; Cholesterol 258mg; Calcium 155mg; Fibre 1.4g; Sodium 116mg

Index

Bibliography

Davidson, Alan. *The Oxford Companion to Food* (Oxford University Press, 1999)
Hartley, Dorothy. *Food in England* (Little, Brown and Company, 1954)
Grigson, Jane. *English Food* (Penguin, 1974)
Mason, Laura with Brown, Catherine. *Traditional Foods of Britain* (Prospect Books, 1999)
Making a Meal of It, Two Thousand Years of English Cookery (English Heritage, 2005)
Spencer, Colin. *British Food, An Extraordinary Thousand Years of History* (Grub Street, 2002)

Author's acknowledgements

The author thanks the following organizations in particular:
www.bbc.co.uk   www.greatbritishkitchen.co.uk